PRAISE FOR THE CIONET COOKBOOK

"Storytelling" is vital in the change journey for Digital Transformation and the 2nd Edition of CIONET's Cookbook is another terrific blend of inspirational stories from fantastic leaders. From tips for reimaging retail to incorporating the latest cyber security practices, the book constitutes a master class in digital leadership for the information age.

Phil Jordan | Group CIO, JS Sainsbury's PLC; Chair, Digital 9 Infrastructure PLC

An extraordinary accomplishment. *CIONET Cookbook: Recipes for Digital Success* goes beyond simply explaining how to best employ digital technology in the workplace to demonstrate how a business's culture must change to fully benefit from digital transformation. Get this book if you are interested in optimising the impact of your enterprise's digital resources.

Rudi Peeters | CEO, Vandersanden

If I had to pick one book to demonstrate how leading organisations are digitally transforming their operations and culture to thrive today this would be it. *CIONET Cookbook: Recipes for Digital Success*, provides a comprehensive picture of the steps digital leaders are taking to traverse the complexity of modern business technology and cook up a winning strategy. A must have for anyone looking to up their game and take an organisation's digital deployments to the next level.

Tarun Kohli | Managing Director, Group Delivery Services, Swiss Re Group & Chairman, Swiss Re Solutions AG (Ltd); ex-CTO of Prudential

Translating advanced technology into performance and competitiveness is the name of the game in today's business world, and the top chefs of the digital kitchen prepare the way for tasty technology treats. If you want to know how these talented cooks write the script for digital success, this is the book for you.

Kurt De Ruwe | CIO, Akzo Nobel

A phenomenal mix of inspirational and practical advice for integrating digital tools into the fabric of an organisation's operations. The top 'chefs' featured in *CIONET Cookbook: Recipes for Digital Success* demonstrate how they prepare their organisations to feast on the digital transformations they cook up. Anyone who is interested in maximising the benefit of today's IT revolution on their organisation should get this book.

Günther Ghijsels | CIO / CDO, Randstad Group, Belgium

How can you best deploy your organisation's technology resources? Read the *CIONET Cookbook* to find out how some of the top digital leaders, master chefs of the digital kitchen, have unlocked the complexity of digital deployments to improve efficiency and enhance organisational culture. The recipes these leaders use are described in detail, making the book both inspirational reading and a template for anyone embarking on their own digital transformation.

Melanie Kehr | Melanie Kehr, Member of the Executive Board (CIO, COO) of KfW

If you want to learn how top digital leaders are guiding their organisations to use the technology to improve productivity and drive innovation, this is the book for you. It persuasively demonstrates that it takes more than simply adopting the latest digital functionality to benefit from them, it also requires an associated change in mindset. This groundbreaking book is a must have for anyone interested in taking their organisation's digital transformation to the next level.

Erwin Verstraelen | Chief Digital Inform. & Innov. Officer, Port of Antwerp-Bruges

Managing the complexity of the modern business world requires a comprehensive, adaptive digital strategy, and this is exactly what the experts featured in the *CIONET Cookbook: Recipes for Digital Success* deliver. These master chefs of the digital kitchen draw on their extensive experience to describe how to optimize your organisation's results. In my view, this book is a must for anyone looking to take their company's digital transformation to the next level.

Mark Foulsham | Chief Operating Officer, Kensington Mortgages

Whether your business is in the midst of digital transformation or simply uses technology for the sake of efficiency, this book can help you optimise your efforts. It features stories of top digital leaders using their 'cooking' skills to bake, broil or steam up tasty results in the form of highly effective, well-integrated technology usage. Whatever the dish served, the result is digital success of the highest level, and these examples make this book absolutely essential for anyone looking to boost productivity.

Geert Standaert | Chief Technology Officer, Proximus

Get the *CIONET Cookbook* 2023 edition now: *Recipes for Digital Success* if you want to learn how leading organisations are successfully navigating their way through digital transformations. Replete with edifying examples, the book is a treasure trove of digital "recipes" for success. From adopting cultural change that embraces technology to effectively employing the latest digital tools, the book covers the full spectrum of techniques for optimizing an organisation's use of technology—an absolute must for organisations transitioning into the fifth revolution

Dr. Bijna Kotak Dasani MBE, FRSA | Top of Fortune India's 2022 Most Dynamic (Business) Personalities List; *www.bijna.com*

CIONET COOKBOOK No.2

RECIPES FOR DIGITAL SUCCESS

Leaders Press

Published in the United States by Leaders Press.
www.leaderspress.com

ISBN 978-1-63735-204-5 (hcv)
ISBN 978-1-63735-202-1 (pbk)
ISBN 978-1-63735-203-8 (eBook)

SIMON & SCHUSTER

Print Book Distributed by Simon & Schuster
1230 Avenue of the Americas
New York, NY 10020

Library of Congress Control Number: 2022922565

MENU

FOREWORD

The pace of digital transformation continues to accelerate rapidly. With a growing emphasis on both customer and employee experience, CIOs are at the forefront of this transformation. They must break down internal barriers and forge deeper connections with external partners. Strategic choices are being made daily about which platforms to adopt at every layer of the technology stack.

Digital leaders recognise that the confluence of so many changes presents a unique set of challenges both to businesses and the IT organisations. For many, heritage applications and associated data remain deeply embedded within the enterprise, creating barriers to modernisation. The skills shortage restricts the pace of change, impacting an organisation's ability to be both innovative and competitive.

Red Hat has been helping customers manage the rapid pace of transformation for nearly three decades. We enable organisations to tap into the innovation engine that is open source, and help them build the skills that help to amplify differentiation and value. Open source as a system for innovation is spreading across industries. It is the ideal way to realise the potential that exists in an organisation providing access to a global community of open source developers, putting innovation in the hands of everyone.

In this second edition of the Cookbook, Red Hat and Intel are delighted to collaborate once again with CIONET to present new recipes for digital success based on TV interviews with top CIOs across Europe and CIONET's recent research. What has become clear to us all is the extraordinary technical and business challenges of the time. This edition provides further insights into the best practices required to flourish in a new digital era.

We believe that this new edition of the cookbook with its exciting recipes and broader insights gathered from the CIONET community will help digital leaders to solve the big issues, both now and for the future.

We hope you enjoy this cookbook.

Hans J. Roth, Senior Vice President & General Manager,
Red Hat Europe, Middle East and Africa

THE MASTER CHEFS

Sam Kini 11

Unilever

Sven Egyedy 15

Federal Foreign Office of Germany

Åshild Hanne Larsen 18

Equinor

Nik Puri 24

FedEx

Guido Lemeire 27

SNCB

Thomas Mannmeusel 30

Webasto

Tomasz Blicharski 33

Żabka Group

Christa Koenen 52

DB Schenker

Michal Paprocki 55

Euroclear

Carsten Trapp 58

Carl Zeiss AG

Breno Gentil 64

HEINEKEN®

Barbara Poli 67

Grandi Navi Veloci

Javier Cabrerizo 71

Prosegur

Gunnar Hellekson 74

Red Hat

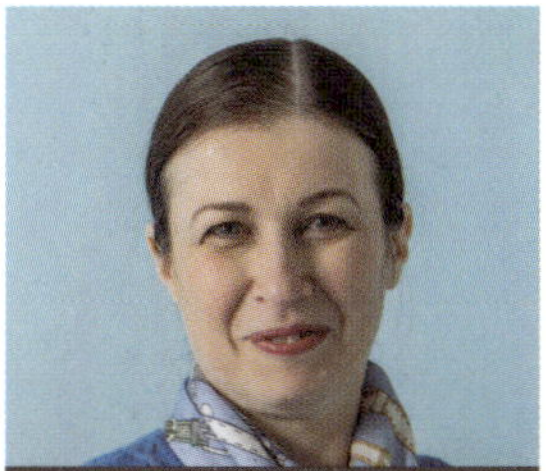

Natasha Davydova 94

Allianz Technology

Stuart Birrell 98

EasyJet

Massimo Rosso 104

RAI

Kristin Lindmark 107

SPP

Marco Moretti 112

A2A

Melissa Evers 115

Intel

INTRODUCTION

Master Chefs in Action

Presenting the Master Chefs of European technology leadership

The transformation of incumbent organisations into digital businesses has thrown a bright spotlight on the role of technology leaders. Now, perhaps more than ever before, private and public sector organisations need CIOs who can help their businesses cope with a complex myriad of challenges. From the shift to hybrid working to wider macro-economic concerns and onto the emergence of new technologies, digital leaders will play a crucial role in helping their organisations to confront the challenges they face and to embrace the new opportunities they unearth.

The good news is that considerable progress in this endeavour is already being made. This Cookbook, the second edition of our guide to technology leadership, presents the recipes for success of CIOs from across Europe. We refer to these pioneers as are our Master Chefs—and our analysis of their work presents what we consider to be the very best of European IT leadership. These Master Chefs, along with those showcased in the first edition of our Cookbook, run technology organisations like five-star restaurants, providing all the IT ingredients for digitally enabled business transformation.

Managing the culinary challenges that lie ahead

When we published the first edition of the CIONET Cookbook, we remarked on the rapid pace of change in the wake of the coronavirus pandemic. Twelve months on and the pace of change is even faster. Complexity is the new business normal. Russia's invasion of Ukraine has had dramatic consequences for energy and food prices. Meanwhile, the end of cheap money has inflated the cost of borrowing. Add in the continued shift to online-everything, the rise of hybrid working and continued fears over environmental catastrophe, and the scale of complexity seems almost unbounded.

After two decades of relative stability, the confluence of changes since the start of this decade has conspired to present senior executives with unprecedented challenges. After speaking with our Master Chefs, the message that emerges is loud and clear: Traditional strategies and mindsets will not help organisations to survive beyond this decade. Leaders must articulate a clear and compelling vision that supports an innovation and growth strategy in a digital economy.

Making that shift, however, is far from easy. Enacting a clear vision for change in the context of economic

uncertainty requires corporate agility, where transformation is taken as a succession of small, incremental steps. The new corporate mantra is all about "sensing and responding" to the external environment. We believe organisations must learn to become organic rather than static if they are to flourish. Successful Master Chefs will deliver organic recipes for tech-enabled change.

The changing role of the Master Chef

The billions of Euros spent on streamlining back-office functions during the past two decades has had little effect when it comes to alleviating sluggish growth and flatlining productivity. The Master Chefs in this Cookbook recognise that IT organisations must rethink their roles, and how they implement technology, in order to overcome the challenges of a new digital era.

The Cookbook exemplifies how Master Chefs develop business architectures and models that align with digital work. Processes are redesigned to provide more compelling experiences to attract and retain profitable customers and talented workers. New digital businesses are created to expand the top line now, as well as providing greater options for future growth.

In all these respects, successful Master Chefs position themselves as integrators by breaking down internal silos and external barriers. They devise new digital architectures and find partners that can facilitate the transition from old to new. To make this change successfully, Master Chefs are cloudifying their platforms and adopting Agile development tools.

But to undertake all these tasks successfully, Master Chefs must prove themselves able and willing to work with their business peers to create technology-enabled solutions to their challenges. The exploding pipeline of new techniques provides plentiful answers to business problems, so long as digital leaders and their executive peers are confident enough to grasp them.

Introducing new ingredients to the Digital Kitchen

As tastes change, so must structures, platforms, and tooling. Making this shift is a radical task, according to the evidence of the recipes in this edition of the Cookbook. We believe four initiatives are key for Master Chefs who are reinventing their Digital Kitchens—the collection of internal and external skills that enable transformation—for a new digital era:

- The addition of software products and services that engenders agility and scalability, instead of an over-reliance on monolithic systems and IT structures
- The cloudification of infrastructures and legacy applications, which opens the prospect for scalable and flexible platforms that support digital business
- The consolidation and standardisation of data resources, together with the application of powerful analytic tools, which enables all parties to have easy access to information assets
- The democratisation of tooling, such as robotic process automation and low code/no code, which enables employees to accelerate the process of digital transformation

Across all these initiatives, successful Master Chefs are reforming and reinvigorating their Digital Kitchens and the culinary offerings they produce for an audience with a sophisticated palate.

Understanding the key attributes of successful Master Chefs

This second edition of the CIONET Cookbook highlights once again how Master Chefs are highly skilled leaders who work with their Digital Kitchens to cook up tantalising dishes that satisfy the business' hunger for digital transformation. More than just being great IT leaders, Master Chefs have a range of innate personal qualities.

Most clearly of all, perhaps, it's important to recognise the humanity of great leaders. Time and again, our Master Chefs use terms like humility, kindness, patience, sensitivity, and openness. Yes, digital leaders are responsible for big budgets and huge change agendas, but success is dependent on the teams they lead. CIOs must make work enjoyable. If you're happy at work as a leader, then it's likely your staff will be too. Self-awareness is crucial for mastering complex situations, so Master Chefs use meditation, mindfulness, and mentorships to stay present and empowered.

Successful CIOs deliver on their promises. However, they achieve great results by working with their teams, not against them. Master Chefs suggest delivery must take place bottom-up rather than top-down to ensure inclusivity. They encourage their staff to be brave and to fail fast without recrimination. They also think about continuous development and find ways to nurture their teams, helping people to grow and learn. Finally, they are inclusive. They build diverse teams with a multitude of experiences, backgrounds, and viewpoints.

Master Chefs also communicate purpose. Technology is at the centre of business change, so everyone in the organisation must understand the impact of digital transformation. Great leaders connect with the rhythm of the business and understand how fast it can travel. To feel comfortable with this cadence, Master Chefs build strong executive partnerships. They communicate effectively and tell stories. They create a strong vision that people want to buy into, making the outcomes of work clear for their teams and the rest of the business.

Finally, in an age of almost constant change, digital leaders are adaptable. They recognise that curiosity and flexibility are essential ingredients for a successful technology career. They keep an attentive eye on new problems to solve and harness innovative solutions from an ecosystem of people and partners. In many ways, great digital leaders act like a sponge. They seek out new knowledge and approaches, surrounding themselves with trusted experts. In short, Master Chefs apply a "can-do" attitude. They always move forward and look to escape their comfort zones whenever they can.

How to use this Cookbook

By drawing out strong use case examples, encapsulated in tasty recipes, we describe how your organisation can create and operate a five-star restaurant and to provide all the ingredients to attract the most discerning diners. The book is divided into three sections that answer these critical questions:

- Section One—What leadership qualities are needed to win the hearts and minds of customers and employees?
- Section Two—How do business strategies and supporting processes need to be transformed to meet the demands of a digital economy?
- Section Three—Where do next-generation infrastructures and digital platforms fit into a digital business and how can data play a defining role?

Our recipes are embellished by the use of Playbooks. These research-based summaries outline best-practice techniques for culinary success across a range of crucial areas, including automation, innovation, data-centricity, and cybersecurity. These Playbooks are based on extensive interviews with the CIONET community and provide new insights into the preparation of five-star cuisine. Now, join us and our Master Chefs as we help you to develop a taste for a new digital era.

SECTION 1

CULTIVATING CULINARY DELIGHTS

★★★★★

"Technology is an important enabler of change; however, people and culture are the essential levers to achieving a truly digital mindset across an entire organisation."

In the first edition of the CIONET Cookbook, we identified five prevailing qualities of leadership that are appropriate for the digital era. These characteristics are curiosity, imagination, purposefulness, authenticity, and dynamism.

Our Master Chefs in this first section of the second edition of the Cookbook are demonstrating a unique combination of these five qualities as they help to reshape their organisations as digital entities and motivate their staff to embrace new ways of operating. We describe these qualities in our first playbook, "The five effective qualities of leadership," which can be found midway through this section.

The seven Master Chefs that we showcase in the first section recognise that technology is an important enabler of change. However, they also appreciate that people and culture are the essential levers to achieving a truly digital mindset across an entire organisation. Well-known management consultant, author, and educator Peter Drucker said, "Culture eats strategy for breakfast." All the Master Chefs adhere to a policy of trust and empowerment that enables individuals and teams to exercise their true talents in pursuit of purposeful change and innovation.

Successful recipes for change must contain a clear and convincing vision for the future that inspires staff at all levels to embark on a journey. The best Master Chefs are storytellers who prepare their organisation and its people for the voyage into digital transformation. At a more practical level, Agile techniques help to convince sceptics that incremental steps, often referred to as sprints, can offer tangible and rapid improvements within and outside the organisation.

The second playbook on "reimagining work" at the end of this section illustrates the profound nature of organisational and cultural change in the modern age, as we emerge from a global pandemic and face new macro-realties such as hybrid working. These organisational and cultural changes include a shift in workflow to focus on the customer experience rather than internal operations, a move from local to global talent sourcing, and a comprehensive rethink about the purpose and design of the office to suit new ways of working.

Our Master Chefs won acclamations from their peers for enabling entire workforces to move safely to their homes within a matter of days during the early stages of the coronavirus pandemic in 2020. Now they must help their organisations to complete the journey to hybrid working. At the same time, these Master Chefs recognise the power of emerging technologies, such as artificial intelligence, machine learning and robotics, to reduce the burden of routine tasks and enrich the work experience. The tantalising prospect of a combined digital and human workforce could be just a few years away.

Sam Kini at Unilever believes innovation can help Unilever solve its business challenges and streamline its structure, with technologies such as artificial intelligence and the metaverse bringing further opportunities for improvements to products and processes. Meanwhile, Sven Egyedy of the Federal Foreign Office of Germany invokes the concept of the North Star to induce a sense of purpose into his organisation. And Åshild Larsen of Equinor states wisely that "you need to strike a delicate balance between optimism and reality." She refers to the famous quote by Abraham Lincoln, suggesting that the best way to predict the future is to create it.

Above all, the seven Master Chefs showcased in the first section of our Cookbook see people and culture as the most important ingredients to their successful change strategies. Let's tuck in.

ONE
LEADERSHIP

The three recipes in this subsection showcase digital leadership at Unilever, the Federal Foreign Office of Germany, and Equinor, Norway's leading oil company. They provide powerful insights into the essential ingredients of leadership as we enter the digital era. In all cases, the Master Chefs at these organisations illustrate how working hand in hand with their business and external partners can position IT as a source of value rather than corporate overhead.

The first critical ingredient for leadership success is an enterprise strategy and architecture that is based on a digital business model. In all three recipes, a data-first principle dominates the agenda, with access to consolidated data that all ecosystem partners can use with speed and simplicity.

The second ingredient is an ability to grasp the opportunities presented by macro-level events, such as how Unilever is using technology to support its sustainability agenda. This approach includes applying blockchain technology to trace the source of ingredients for main product lines to create sustainable supply chains. Another example is the timely response to the coronavirus pandemic by the Federal Foreign Office, which mobilised resources and overcame organisational inertia.

Finally, the third ingredient as illustrated by Equinor, is a capacity to apply new technologies, such as artificial intelligence and fibre optics, in an attempt to solve a range of traditional business challenges that includes minimising mechanical problems associated with offshore drilling and optimising valuable energy resources.

For all three Master Chefs, effective digital leadership is all about setting a clear vision, creating a compelling case for action, and trusting the IT, business, and external resources to access and deliver great solutions to disparate business challenges.

Unilever

Tackling complexity to enable transformation

Ingredients

- Sustainability must be included in a common purpose
- Technology and process complexity carry a hidden burden for the organisation and in turn, create capacity for greater differentiation and innovation
- The power of enquiry and learning provide the fastest route to digital leadership success

Preparing the dish

Sam Kini is global CIO at Unilever. Having graduated with a degree in business administration, she spent the early part of her career in the telecommunications sector, heading technology transformation for Virgin Media in the UK and acting as CIO for Telenet in Belgium. More recently, she was CD&IO for EasyJet. She joined Unilever in January 2021, becoming global CIO in May 2022.

Unilever is a global consumer goods company headquartered in London. The company employs more than 150,000 colleagues, operates in 190 countries, and 3.4 billion people every day use their products, with their global brands including Dove, Hellmann's, Magnum ice cream, and OMO.

Undertaking a global transformation

In July 2022, Unilever changed its business model from a matrix structure, to being organised around five distinct business groups: Home Care, Nutrition, Ice Cream, Health & Wellbeing, and Personal Care.

"Design once and deploy everywhere."

Sam Kini, CIO, Unilever

Scan code to watch the full interview.

Each business group is fully responsible and accountable for its strategy, growth, and profit delivery globally.

This operating model change has been accompanied by a CEO-led commitment to pursue a common purpose that includes improving the health of the planet, improving health and wellbeing, and contributing to a more socially-inclusive world. Unilever believes companies with purpose last, brands with purpose grow, and people with purpose thrive.

One example of how Unilever is using technology to support its sustainability agenda is a joint venture with Google that is employing a geospatial platform to identify the effects of deforestation due to the use of palm oil. The company aims to be deforestation-free by 2023. The venture is also applying blockchain technology to trace the source of ingredients for Unilever's main product lines to create sustainable supply chains.

Helping to enact the new corporate strategy

Sam believes technology is an essential ingredient in creating a simplified corporate structure and enacting the company's new vision around a common purpose. The technology organisation is playing a lead role in providing access to emerging technologies, such as blockchain, that can help the company reach its sustainability goals. Automation at scale, meanwhile, is being used to drive efficiencies, process improvements, and enrich the roles that Unilever staff play, allowing people to spend more time improving products and services.

Sam's main priority is to simplify Unilever's technology landscape, so that it can be used to enable the company's new global structure based on supporting growth in its five business groups. She is focused on tackling complexity and simplification, whilst reinvesting back into innovation and digital transformation.

Sam's mantra is "design once and deploy everywhere." Her team also uses the metaphor of reducing body mass index to describe their aims for digital transformation. This work involves a wholesale consolidation of technology applications, driven by a unifying framework, that will allow the business to use technology to increase its speed and agility.

Introducing a slimmed down approach for ERP

Unilever has spent many years consolidating its various ERP systems into a unified SAP platform. The company now has just four SAP instances. However, Sam believes further modernisation is necessary to help technology serve the company's global brands and growth effectively. Her team has also instituted an aggressive move to the cloud, with the aim of transferring 95% of applications by the end of 2022.

Sam is also aiming to shrink the company's core SAP system to a centralised financial layer based on S/4HANA. She will supplement this core with Software as a Service (SaaS) applications across key areas, such as HR and CRM. This shift to the cloud will improve flexibility and accelerate global standardisation. It will allow Unilever to escape the rigid structures of traditional ERP systems and support an ongoing move towards best-of-breed SaaS services.

Refreshing the kitchen

Sam manages a global technology team across multiple geographies including UK, Singapore, Bangalore, and Brazil. Guided by her operating principle of "utilising the power of one, with targeted solutions for the five business groups," Sam runs a large central team that has responsibility for setting the overall technology strategy and direction for Unilever and running all global platforms and technology.

To reduce complexity further, Sam is focused on consolidating vendor relationships, especially for service integration. She believes moving to a handful of strategic partnerships will reduce costs and increase collaboration. She is also keen to bring as much intellectual property as possible in-house to encourage innovation and competitive differentiation.

Sam believes innovation can help Unilever solve its business challenges and streamline its structure. She also believes that artificial intelligence and the metaverse bring further opportunities for product and process innovation.

Defining the qualities of a Master Chef

Sam places business firmly ahead of technology. Her goal is to bring a digital vision to Unilever and to work with the C-suite to solve business challenges. At the technology coalface, she is keen to eliminate hierarchy and ensure everyone has a voice. She wants to create a fearless technology organisation that embraces global transformation projects. Her message to incoming talent is that Unilever operates with unrivalled scale, providing diverse career choices and great opportunities.

Sam's curiosity and questioning has always guided her well in her own career and she has a deep desire that all young aspiring leaders ask lots of questions and challenge the status quo.

Federal Foreign Office of Germany

Genesis of a digital revolution within government

Ingredients

- Your leadership role cannot be delegated. Take full responsibility for it
- Informed decisions need to be based on the best information available at the time
- Your team deserves empowerment and trust. You should consider yourself an equal member

Preparing the dish

Dr. Sven Egyedy is the CDO of the Federal Foreign Office of Germany. Having dedicated his career to working in the public sector, Sven believes that citizens are entitled to the most reliable and efficient services that the government can provide and afford. He argues that digital solutions play a crucial role in service delivery and can help government organisations reduce gaps in service provision. Having gained experience in a variety of government roles, which included a stint in nuclear fusion, Sven's mantra is to steer carefully towards what he calls "the North Star" by applying a disciplined approach to all the work his team performs.

Germany's Federal Foreign Office acts as a global organisation, comprising 240 physical stations with 13,000 staff, including embassies and consulates. This organisation requires the latest technology if it is to be efficient and effective. Recent events, such as the repatriation of 240,000 German citizens during the coronavirus pandemic and the advent of data-driven decision making, have created new challenges and opportunities.

Using agile techniques to respond to the COVID-19 crisis

The German Government instructed the Foreign Office to manage the repatriation of 240,000 German citizens living abroad in just five weeks during March 2020. While the government had a comprehensive list of affected citizens, there wasn't any surplus data to help tackle this unique challenge. Sven immediately convened a crisis team and commissioned a critical code review to support the repatriation. The first attempt at this process was unsuccessful, as was the second. These failures left the team with just 24 hours to develop an entirely new approach.

Activating all available resources, Sven called on strategic business partners such as SAP as well as the government's Crisis Response Centre. He adopted a radical method based on Agile techniques to develop a productive system in hours rather than days or months. Starting at 5 p.m., with a team of 10 people, Sven undertook a series of two-hour sprints throughout the night to develop a minimum viable product. By morning, the task was complete. Checks for data protection and security were then undertaken at speed. The project's success was inspiring for the 350 staff that report to Sven.

The rapid response to repatriation has now become a valuable illustration of how Agile techniques might be applied as part of a broader digital transformation of the ministry. Sven recognises that several elements will need to be in place to guarantee successful outcomes. These include a proven architectural framework, a motivated team, as well as clear goals and objectives. Success will also require a culture that tolerates failure—including as a means to improve and to learn.

Introducing data-driven decision making

Fast-developing global crises are always a significant management concern. These crises can develop at exponential speed and generate large volumes of data that are difficult to capture and handle. The German Government was very aware that it needed a more proactive approach to help detect and then prevent crises. It turned to Sven's department to support the development of a tool that could be used by diplomatic staff to anticipate impending crises.

To deliver this digital system, known as PREVIEW, Sven and his team adopted existing frameworks. For example, they built a public cloud to store and analyse vast amounts of data held by government entities. Sven then recognised PREVIEW

"Take full responsibility for your leadership role—don't delegate this duty."

Sven Egyedy, CDO, Federal Foreign Office of Germany

Scan code to watch the full interview.

could be the precursor to a new data-driven environment across other ministries. This task required agility and scalability.

Sven was aware that this technology-enabled development would require a fundamental change in culture. Many senior diplomats rely on traditional decision-making approaches and are suspicious of new techniques such as artificial intelligence. Yet Sven highlighted the potential benefits of a data-driven approach. Today, his team's work in support of PREVIEW has led to major changes in how the Foreign Office performs its tasks, which is stimulating a digital revolution across the German Government.

Defining the qualities of a Master Chef

Successful leaders in the public sector must meet tough targets while balancing administrative and political pressures. Effective civil service leadership is often more complex than in the private sector, where a profit-based mentality prevails over other considerations. Sven's way of dealing with this complexity is to develop "the North Star," a seven-year strategy which contains broader organisational objectives linked to the evolving requirements of citizens and ministers. He implements the strategy by adopting a set of key performance indicators and processes that must be met in order to deliver the desired outcomes. This approach enables IT to measure its contribution to the organisation in a tangible way and helps protect the team from political interference.

Sven's leadership style combines a long-term vision with hands-on intervention. He is keen to empower his team, but also recognises that complex problems require a deep-dive approach to management. His broad education, which encompasses law, technology, and a Ph.D. in social sciences, gives him knowledge to support his team. Sven is willing to bring in external expertise when required, while at the same time recognising that a leader becomes responsible for all decisions that are taken. Leaders cannot delegate their responsibilities.

A key success factor for his ministry is attracting top talent. Sven meets new entrants and shares his views about the purpose of public service organisations. He meets with recruits after a six-month period to reinforce this message. Even when staff members choose to leave the Foreign Office, they often later return as they appreciate the excellent team spirit and clear goals that are maintained within his department.

Equinor

Harnessing the power of technology

Ingredients

- Technologies such as fibre optics and artificial intelligence bring new sources of value
- Consolidated data reservoirs help to reduce operational risk and optimise yield
- Optimism is a powerful asset for any digital leader in today's uncertain environment

Preparing the dish

Åshild Hanne Larsen is Vice President of Subsurface Excellence and Digital at Equinor, formerly known as Statoil. Åshild graduated with a Master in languages and education and has also completed an MBA. She started her career as a catering assistant at Statoil and climbed the career ladder to become an HR executive. She was appointed Senior Vice President and Group CIO for Statoil in 2015. After 6 years as CIO, she moved to a subsurface Vice President role in 2021, with global responsibility for the subsurface technology and digital portfolio, data and information, toolbox, and work processes, as well as quality assurance and control.

Equinor is an international energy company headquartered in Stavanger, Norway. The firm's origins date back to 1972, when it was established following the discovery of large oil and gas reservoirs on the Norwegian continental shelf. Today, Norway is one of the world's most productive petroleum provinces and a test lab for technology development. Equinor employs 22,000 staff and operates in 30 countries. Åshild is proud that her organisation serves the energy needs of over 170 million people worldwide and is a front runner in promoting renewable energy.

"The best way to predict the future is to create it."

Åshild Hanne Larsen, Vice President of Subsurface Excellence and Digital, Equinor

Scan code to watch the full interview.

Driving transformation and value creation through IT

When Åshild became Group CIO seven years ago, the IT function was considered more of a commodity and cost for the business rather than a strategic value generator. There was significant pressure to cut IT spending rather than to increase it. Åshild, however, was convinced that technology could be used to help solve key business challenges and open up new opportunities. Together with her team, she took a bet on developing OMNIA, Equinor's cloud-based data platform, recognising that access to data could be used to reduce risk and produce a competitive advantage.

She also launched the cross-business Go Digital initiative to identify business challenges and opportunities that could be solved by technology and designed a corporate-wide digital academy to ensure development of the capabilities needed for the future. Finally, she was the architect behind a strategic partnership with the tech giant Microsoft that not only resulted in 2 new data centre regions in Norway but boosted the entire Norwegian tech and supplier ecosystem. These are all strong examples of how IT added fresh value to the business across technology, data, and people, under Åshild's visionary leadership.

Reducing risk, optimising yield

In her current role in the subsurface, Åshild and her team run a big portfolio of digital projects aimed at reducing risk, improving efficiency, and creating value. Since the subsurface is extremely data rich, cleaning, liberating, and analysing data is at the core of their efforts. The company's Subsurface Data Lake project aims to make data available for analytics anytime and anywhere, providing a holistic understanding of underwater oil and gas reservoirs.

A second project focuses on utilising fibre optics data to improve production and safety. Fibre optics are placed along many of Equinor's wells to gather data. On the Johan Sverdrup field on the Norwegian continental shelf, an interrogator is placed on top that sends laser pulses down the cable, records what is returned and converts that into either sound or temperature data. Traditionally, the process of viewing this data took two or three weeks and involved flying hard drives to shore via helicopter. Now, the amount of data is the equivalent of 10,000 Netflix movies per second and it takes two or three seconds to livestream it for real-time monitoring. By using software and machine learning, production from the wells can be optimised, and safety can be improved through fast detection of issues.

Their AIM project uses rules-based gamification AI to find the optimal trajectory for a robot finding its way through a maze. AIM allows users to automatically screen many more solutions, improving efficiency, safety, and recovery, and it can even unlock paths that were impossible to calculate manually. Engineers can now select from the best auto-generated drilling trajectories and perform their tasks with greater speed and accuracy, which drives efficiency, supports faster decision-making processes, and creates higher yields on investment.

Demonstrating digital leadership

Having worked across a range of functions during her ascent to executive roles in the company, Åshild has an intimate connection with the business requirements of Equinor. She says modern CIOs must be more than just excellent technologists. Effective digital leaders are good translators and are able to sell opportunities to their peers across the organisation. Åshild's strong network and her awareness of the various functions of the business held her in good stead when she became CIO in 2015. This knowledge enabled her to connect business and IT in new ways and create a better understanding of business needs and how they could be addressed by utilising new technology-driven opportunities.

Åshild has actively utilised Equinor's three principles for successful leadership—shape, empower, and deliver—during her long career with the company. First, focusing on new opportunities will help shape the future of the business. She believes technology must work hand in hand with human effort to reach new digital frontiers. Second, the team must be empowered and leadership must be clear about what the IT organisation can offer. Third, see through on your promises so you can be seen as a trusted deliverer. She believes this concentration on delivery is especially important in a strong engineering environment.

Defining the qualities of a Master Chef

Åshild equates technology with progress, but she is careful to strike a balance between optimism and reality. Having risen from humble beginnings within the organisation, Åshild has learnt to value every individual regardless of status. This quality enables her to treat people with the respect they deserve. She is a great believer in continuous development as her team navigates a rapidly changing business environment. As Equinor shifts out of its traditional offshore exploration business into international markets and products, she recognises that while some of Equinor's foundational competencies are still relevant, the company will also need to attract and build a new type of expertise.

Åshild's mantra is, "What doesn't kill you will make you stronger." She has a firm belief that digital leaders hold a privileged position from which to help shape the future. She quotes Abraham Lincoln who said, "The best way to predict the future is to create it." Åshild advises aspiring leaders to avoid becoming a perfectionist and to say "yes" to every opportunity. She recognises that new opportunities have arisen in many unfamiliar areas during her own career. However, taking on these fresh openings—including becoming CIO—has helped Åshild stretch her capabilities and flourish professionally.

Amberjack ceviche

Serves 1 portion

- 70g of raw fresh amberjack, cut into cubes
- 50g of red and yellow cherry tomatoes
- 20g of red bell pepper
- 20g of red onion
- 1 avocado diced
- 1 small jalapeno, seeds removed and diced
- 10g cilantro chopped
- 5–6 leaves of mint
- 1 lime
- 1 Tbsp olive oil
- smoked salt & ground black pepper to taste

This light, fresh, and citrusy amberjack ceviche recipe can be enjoyed all year round as a starter. Variations on ceviche are endless. It can be made with any type of fish, scallops or shrimp and any vegetables such as radishes, cucumbers, artichokes, capers, and celery. Fruits like pineapple, green apple and orange are a nice addition. Just pick your favourite seafood and vegetables and give this recipe a try.

For a colourful effect, choose different coloured tomatoes, cleaned, and pressed together in a tomato juicer or crush them in a mixer. Filter them and let it set for 30 minutes to deepen the flavours of the purees.

Cut the Amberjack fillet into regular bite size cubes. Season it with smoked salt, olive oil, lime skin and juice then stir well. The lime juice is "cooking" the fish, so make sure it coats all the fish. Let it sit for 30 minutes and check that the inside of the fish is firm with the same colour all the way through to make sure it's properly "cooked."

In the meantime, cut into small dices the red onions, peppers, jalapeños, cilantro, and avocado. Season the mixture with salt, olive oil, lime, and mint leaves. Pour the tomato purees into your favourite serving dish. Add the marinated fish cubes and decorate with little mint leaves for the final touches.

If you are making ceviche ahead of time, do everything as instructed above except for the avocado and cilantro. Gently fold the diced avocado with the cilantro into the mixture before serving.

Ceviche is best when fresh, so don't let it sit for more than a couple hours. Consume immediately!

The favourite dish of Breno Gentil

TWO
CULTURE AND PEOPLE

For the four Master Chefs featured in this subsection, the ascendancy of technology and its effect on organisational mindset and culture is a foremost challenge. These four leaders all meet this issue head-on. The four Master Chefs demonstrate an ability to bring the rest of their organisation along for the journey into a new digital age. This transition involves the combination of a unique set of ingredients that includes cross-functional collaboration on the inside and co-creation with customers and partners on the outside.

FedEx has adopted a radical business model based on data-first and Industry 4.0 principles. Sharing data across the entire supply chain brings speed and nimbleness to connected partners in automotive, healthcare, and other sectors.

SNCB has used the voice of the customer and employee to transform the perception of IT from a problem area into a source of business value. By using a process of constant iteration, the IT organisation has created a series of "bright spots" that help to inspire confidence in technology.

Webasto has helped to close the artificial separation of IT and business operations. This gap has been bridged by developing a group-wide programme of successful process integration across functional and geographic boundaries that it refers to as the Global Process Organisation.

Żabka Polska has adopted a bimodal approach to business transformation. One team has applied new technologies to the existing retail business in order to stabilise core revenues and profits. A second team has built entirely new revenue streams around the core by engaging a new generation of consumers through the development of mobile applications.

These four businesses have very different approaches. However, there is one common recipe that is key to success in all these organizations: the constant need to communicate success and stick to promises.

FedEx

Leading with body, mind, and soul

Ingredients

- The Body: A strong and enduring corporate culture that engages all members of staff across more than 220 countries and territories where FedEx operates
- The Mind: A core business architecture promoting simplicity, with freedom at the edge to deliver speed and nimbleness to customers
- The Soul: A data-first vision that enables the organisation to compete effectively with digital natives

Preparing the dish

Founded in 1971, FedEx operates across more than 220 countries and territories, employing half a million people. Success is based on a differentiated culture that Nik Puri, Senior Vice President IT for FedEx Express Solutions International, refers to as "the secret sauce" of the firm. FedEx must also keep a watchful eye on industry disruptors, such as digital natives, that could challenge its position as a leader in the industry.

To stay ahead, FedEx applies a first-to-market mindset that emphasizes speed over size. At the epicentre of this approach are customers and their fresh demands in key areas, such as global visibility of supply chains and home deliveries. Bringing the voice of the customer into every conversation helps maintain alertness and continuous innovation.

Readying FedEx for Industry 4.0

A combination of factors galvanised FedEx to adopt a radical business model based on data-first and Industry 4.0 principles. The acquisition of TNT in 2016 presented

"The most important ingredients for a successful transformation are people and culture rather than process and technology."

Nik Puri, Senior Vice President IT, FedEx

Scan code to watch the full interview.

a one-time opportunity to reshape global operations, with the pandemic in 2020 providing further incentive to accelerate these developments. In Nik's words, "the future arrived early" by compressing three years of progress into three months.

FedEx adopted a three-step approach to transformation. The first step following the TNT acquisition was to stabilise the environment, ensuring promised synergies were delivered, such as back-office efficiencies. The second more fundamental step was to adopt a digital strategy for the merged entity that included applying data-first operating processes across the supply chain, underpinning key functions with Software as a Service (SaaS) applications, and opening application programming interfaces to give visibility to customers. The final step was introducing new, value-based capabilities for customers to stay ahead of competitors.

Reinventing the business model

FedEx's data-first model propels the company into the digital age, enabling it to compete head-on with digital natives. Sharing data across the entire supply chain brings speed and nimbleness to connected partners in the automotive, healthcare, and other sectors. It also allows FedEx to compete effectively in the business-to-consumer space, which "brought hope to the public" during the coronavirus pandemic.

Nik says the most important ingredients for a successful transformation are people and culture rather than process and technology. FedEx has introduced a philosophy of learning and caring to affect change across its global workforce. An emphasis on a learning mindset helps all staff to understand the new techniques and partnerships of modern business. Leaders who value caring create consensus around the firm's vision and reduce anxiety associated with large-scale change.

Senior executives who lead change must be accessible and highly visible to management teams and front-line staff. FedEx expects executives to demonstrate leadership by being at the forefront of change practices. For Nik, this leadership means engaging more than 2,000 internal IT staff and a similar number of external contractors.

Adopting a data-first philosophy

The founder of FedEx, Frederick W. Smith, stated in the 1970s that "the information about the package is just as important as the package itself." This awareness has helped place data at the centre of FedEx's strategy and operating procedures. Traditional operating models have used data to look backward, which Nik believes is throwing the data away as "exhaust fumes." At FedEx, data is the fuel that powers FedEx's decision-making processes.

A new wave of technologies, from drones to autonomous vehicles, and onto the Internet of Things, artificial intelligence, and software robots, means data must be at the core of business architecture. Take embedded intelligence in moving vehicles, which produces petabytes of information to affect business decisions in real-time. Any firms that want to exploit this resource must embrace digitisation. To emphasise the importance of its data-first strategy, FedEx Dataworks, a new FedEx operating company, was created to provide data-centred logistics solutions to the market.

Reorganising the IT kitchen

The importance of information to FedEx is demonstrated by the fact that Nik's boss, the Group CIO, reports directly to the FedEx Executive Chairman alongside the CEO. The company's IT model is federal, with 10 senior IT executives operating across regions and business divisions. This community is bound together by a single enterprise architecture at the core of the global business that enables interoperability between systems. Funding for other projects is at the edge to encourage innovation and agility within national markets.

Nik has helped oversee the virtualisation of 80% of computers and applications across the globe and the adoption of co-located rather than private data centres. Standardised software has been rolled out to all 750 European logistics stations, with reliability at 99.99%. The implementation of a hybrid-working strategy, meanwhile, necessitated the provision of 100,000 virtual private network connections during and after the pandemic.

Defining the qualities of a Master Chef

Joining FedEx in 1999, Nik has filled multiple management roles across the business that have rounded his executive experiences. Yet, he sees himself as a servant rather than a boss. He aims to set the vision for his IT staff, provide the necessary funding, and empower the team. Then, he "steps out of the way." He sets the strategy but relies on his team to respond to local conditions on the battlefield.

In line with FedEx's corporate philosophy of learning and caring, Nik believes personal authenticity is a critical asset as a leader. He uses "3Fs" to describe his personal leadership style: Faith in yourself and how you live your life; Family orientation to exemplify work/life balance; and FedEx, which illustrates a passion for your work. Nik believes that body, mind, and soul should be dedicated to creating new generations of employees and managers who enjoy what they are doing and aim to make the world a better place.

SNCB

Putting customers at the centre of a business transformation journey

> **Ingredients**
>
> - Successful CIOs state what they want, they repeat the message, and stick to the promise
> - "Bright spots," which are solutions to big issues that show the benefits of digitization, must be the focus
> - The next challenge needs to be in view always—there's no problem for which there is no solution

Preparing the dish

A marketeer by education, Guido Lemeire is an IT leader who focuses on the customer. He cut his technological teeth in the fast-moving telecommunications sector, where he used his marketing skills to develop high-quality products. One example of his pioneering approach came during his time at broadband provider Telenet, where he created an in-house web-agency in just two years. He has continued to embrace new challenges, including a move to the finance sector in 2014. Three years later, he joined SNCB, the National Railway Company of Belgium, becoming CIO in 2018.

SNCB's 18,000 employees support the transportation of 250 million citizens on rail lines across Belgium on an annual basis. Guido provides a broad range of IT services to the organisation—from traditional infrastructure to applications and onto building-management services—through Ypto, which is a 100%-owned SNCB company. Ypto employs 300 IT professionals and 300 consultants.

In early 2019, Guido created a strategic partnership with Tata Consultancy Services, which added an additional 300 experts to the IT organisation.

Building a new approach to IT

Guido inherited an organisation with a high turnover of personnel—30% of staff left during the previous three years. In terms of IT, Guido describes the situation he inherited as "level zero" on the Capability Maturity Model Integration (CMMI) model. Guido saw boosting this status as a big opportunity: "It allows you to bring an organisation from being a risk to a trusted co-creator that can digitalise the SNCB—and that's exactly what we did."

By May 2019, his team had built the foundations for change—an on-demand infrastructure using a cloud-first policy allied to a brand-new data centre. They then migrated 500 applications to the cloud by June 2020. During this time, Guido also had to achieve organisational transformation, which he says was the biggest challenge: "You need to turn the mind of people and a perception that IT is a problem towards a sense that they can contribute and make a difference. We wanted to create a customer-oriented IT organisation."

Developing trust in the approach

Crucial to Guido's success was a new mission statement he used from May 2018: "We wanted to be the co-creator of the digitisation of the SNCB applying IT best practices." As a marketer, he recognises business leaders often need to repeat the same message six or seven times to build understanding. He believes this focus on constant communication is underestimated by many CIOs. IT leaders must state what they want, repeat it continually, and stick to the promise.

Guido says the key to his success at SNCB is addressing business challenges in an iterative way. He gives the example of using digitisation to improve operational processes of train drivers. Guido and his team spent time with drivers and created a user group to understand their challenges. They created "bright spots," which are solutions to critical issues that show the benefits of digitisation. In just 18 months, the train driver experience was fully digitalised, with a transfer from paper-based processes to insight-driven experiences for security, staffing, and planning on a handheld device.

"Great responsibility brings great accountability."

Guido Lemiere, CIO, SNCB

Scan code to watch the full interview.

Moving forward at pace

Guido used a similar approach to deal with the challenges of external customers. Working in close collaboration with marketing and sales, his IT team ran a series of user groups with passengers. They discovered their concerns and demands. This data informed their digitisation programmes, once again creating a series of bright spots that could be industrialised. The team created a new web site, a mobile app, and a route planner, which was enriched with data from other transport services. Guido's team also developed a range of flexible ticketing options for commuting in the post-COVID age.

Guido says the journey to digitisation continues at pace. He estimates SNCB is now at CMMI level two with an ambition to reach a higher level every 18 months. Those stretch targets place pressure on the IT organisation, yet it's a destination he's going to reach by developing a process-driven organisation that focuses on continuous improvement in the way it works. The goal is to create a fully Agile organisation at level four of CMMI maturity.

Building a customer data platform

Guido says the key to delivering great data-led services for customers is focusing on benefits. He says the data platform his team is building is part of a wider ecosystem. SNCB has an open data interface where it provides information to third parties that want to develop applications. The firm also builds relationships with external organisations, such as travel agencies and other transport specialists.

The aim is to create an ecosystem that allows SNCB to move into new areas quickly. Guido says he's impatient by nature and is always looking for the next challenge: "There's no problem for which there is no solution." Yet the result of this proactivity is clear—SNCB creates new, inspiring initiatives. Staff turnover, which once stood at 30%, has been just 5% for the past 12 months. Guido attracts top talent by highlighting how transformative work will have a daily impact on 250 million people.

Defining the qualities of a Master Chef

CIOs in traditional sectors such as rail are still often preoccupied with technology. Guido says CIOs must recognise that technology is simply a lever to achieve business transformation. His role is to establish realistic but ambitious goals for the team. He sets guidelines and ensures staff keep the long-term strategy in mind on a daily basis: "Set out a strategy, stick to it, and ensure it's being executed."

IT staff must remember, says Guido, that great responsibility brings great accountability. He delegates responsibility to his senior team members, but he expects them to deliver results. Guido believes his board perceives him to be an impatient but ambitious business leader: "What gives me professional satisfaction is having a complex challenge, realising it, and setting down the result."

Guido left SNCB to become the Industry leader National Critical Infrastructure Western Europe with Microsoft in Dec 2022.

Webasto Group

Where IT and Business are like Batman and Robin

Ingredients

- "Digital" is just one element of any successful business. To be effective, CIOs must understand the business in its entirety and move IT out of the technology silo
- The role of the CIO today has evolved away from internal process automation. It is now about integrating the many working parts of a business
- Leadership is about making those around you successful, be they colleagues or members of your family

Preparing the dish

Thomas Mannmeusel is Group CIO of Webasto and, in addition, leads a global cross-functional team for process optimization (GPO). His academic research in business administration, and a subsequent Ph.D. in business informatics, led him away from engineering at Infineon and into a senior IT position when he joined Webasto in 2009. It was an opportune time to make the change because of a recession in Europe. One of his guiding principles is that organisations are most open to change during a crisis, which is why he finds such phases rather encouraging.

The Webasto Group, a 100-year-old German company employing 16,000 staff, develops and produces innovative roof systems, heating and cooling solutions, as well as charging stations and battery systems for electric vehicles (EVs). Webasto is privately owned and encourages a continuous search for new products and revenue sources, including EV charging stations.

"My greatest fear in business is to become irrelevant."

Thomas Mannmeusel, Group CIO, Webasto Group

Scan code to watch the full interview.

Building a Global Process Organisation

One of Thomas's first observations when entering his CIO role was the artificial separation between the IT function and the rest of the business. He took up the challenge and reengineered the business to introduce a Global Process Organisation (GPO) that was populated by a team of cross-functional experts drawn from finance, human resources, procurement, operations, research and development, and sales.

Through the GPO, Thomas developed an approach that crossed organisational boundaries and encompassed the full stack of technologies to run an automotive supplier. He used this framework to break down functional silos. The outcomes were significant. Webasto benefited from a 30% reduction of time and effort to integrate newly acquired entities into the group or to establish new plants. The creation of the GPO coincided with the emergence of e-mobility. This area of business offered Webasto opportunities for revenue growth, which were accelerated by the company's new focus on processes.

Developing a charging point for electric vehicles

In 2018, Webasto started providing charging points for electrical vehicle (EV) owners. This new business required a radical transition from a focus on mechanical parts to electrical components and software-based services. It also meant the firm had to develop sales channels directly to the end customer as well as via resellers.

In a joint effort with all relevant functions, the team developed a digital platform that allowed Webasto to launch a set of new charging stations for the German annual automotive trade show in just four months including installation services. This successful launch illustrated how a cross-functional team and tight integration of IT and the rest of the business delivers beneficial outcomes.

Combining engineering and operations

Webasto recognised it would need to integrate engineering and operations more closely if it was going to develop software-based products and services for EVs. Thomas knew one common ERP system across the group would provide the platform for integration, enriched by a common engineering application stack, including Product Lifecycle Management (PLM) and Computer-Aided Design (CAD) Systems as well as a globally harmonised Manufacturing

Execution System (MES). Data could be harmonised and shared between functional teams to create efficiencies across the global supply chain. The platform could also be used to foster digital services that could generate new sources of revenue.

Other developments have had an impact too. The introduction of augmented reality (AR) illustrated how a common platform could support joined-up engineering and operational activities. Remote teams now use AR to install new assets across the globe and support product launches. This success whetted the business appetite for further digitisation.

Changing the IT operating model

Thomas believes the most valuable contribution a CIO can make is to integrate operational processes across functional boundaries. To achieve this goal, he's created a networked IT organisation with a central core of 100 staff, and four regional units with a total staff of 200. The heads of applications and infrastructure are located at the centre to set standards and preserve data harmony. Regional staff contribute directly to business value at the local operating level.

Historically, IT was concerned with internal process automation. Today, Thomas says the wide range of publicly available Software as a Service products means the role of IT has changed. Modern IT is all about integrating a multitude of off-the-shelf components that the businesses need to be competitive. On such a common platform, IT should provide data management services that are transforming the vast amount of data into actionable insights. He believes IT should provide the digital expertise to help the business take advantage of innovative technologies, such as the Internet of Things (IoT), AR, big data, machine learning, or blockchain.

The transition to integrated operational processes at Webasto is being accompanied by a gradual migration from traditional waterfall methods to a new era of Agile developments. Agile provides an incremental approach to IT programmes that suits fast-changing business requirements. Thomas increasingly uses sprints and minimum viable products to demonstrate value to his business partners.

Defining the qualities of a Master Chef

CIOs and their teams must be neutral and trusted by all parties. Thomas' personal style is to be open, honest, and transparent. He relies on facts rather than instincts to make tough decisions and says he and his staff must learn from their mistakes. This approach has a strong parallel with "The Toyota Way," which is a set of principles and behaviours that empowers people at every level to constantly challenge and improve their work environment.

Thomas says that besides excellent leadership and interesting career models, the key to recruiting and developing top talent is to be flexible about location. Webasto's head office is in Munich, which is home to high-tech firms such as Google, Microsoft, and several DAX giants. Rather than competing with firms that offer top salaries, Thomas sources talent from a wider geographical pool.

As a CIO, Thomas is keen to help all his staff grow and become successful. He embraces change, and the associated challenges that come with it. As Thomas says: "My greatest fear in business is to become irrelevant."

Żabka Group

Re-inventing retail through digital transformation

Ingredients

- The core must be modernised using data analytics to deliver operational efficiencies
- "The new" should be created around the core by employing emerging technologies, such as robotics
- Quick action and a growth mindset are required if you want to become a digital leader

Preparing the dish

Tomasz Blicharski is the Executive Vice President of the Management Board of Żabka Group, and Managing Director of Żabka Future, the organisational unit responsible for searching and creating businesses that aim to develop Żabka Group. With a master's in finance, Tomasz completed postgraduate research at Stanford University and then joined Mid Europa Partners, a private equity firm in London. Before taking up his current position, he simultaneously held two posts: Vice President of the Management Board of Żabka Polska for Development (since 2017) and Vice President of the Management Board of Żabka Polska for Finance (since 2015). He has been involved with Żabka Polska since 2011, as a member of the Board of Directors. Tomasz has created a team of people responsible for researching and developing new business areas and technological solutions meeting the challenges the industry faces.

Żabka Group is the ultimate convenience ecosystem that aims to make people's lives easier. Accompanying consumers at every moment of the day, freeing up their time through the possibility of convenient grocery shopping, having a hot meal on the go, sending a package, withdrawing cash, or taking advantage of a dietary catering with delivery. Żabka is one of the most recognizable brands in Poland, with nearly three million customers using their services daily. Based in Poland, Żabka is a chain of over 8,700 modern convenience stores. More than 15.5 million customers live less than 500 metres from their nearest store. Żabka was founded by a Polish entrepreneur in 1998 and was acquired by CVC Capital Partners in 2017.

Optimising the core business

Following acquisition by CVC, the new management team at Żabka focused on ensuring the retailer stayed relevant in a fast-changing sector. The Board took a series of trips, including Silicon Valley, Mexico, and South-East Asia, to assess retail trends around the globe. They concluded Żabka would need to play at the top of its game to succeed and decided full-scale digital transformation was required.

Tomasz could see his investors needed great results quickly, so he and the team applied data analytics, artificial intelligence (AI), and machine learning to the core business. This approach enabled them to optimise prices, identify new store locations, and adjust the assortment of products offered in-store to match local consumer preferences.

The impact of digitisation was immediate, and the business rapidly turned a corner, enabling it to expand rapidly. This growth fed investor confidence and helped to inspire the workforce. Tomasz's use of AI and machine learning to locate new stores gave franchisees the confidence to know they were acquiring profitable businesses.

Developing a consumer app

As part of its ongoing digital transformation, Żabka was eager to engage younger consumers and to increase customer loyalty and basket size. Tomasz commissioned the development of an app, known as Żappka, that would offer new services, such as loyalty points and Żappka Pay.

The app was an instant success. To date, the Żappka app has been downloaded by over 10 million users. Consumers can use the loyalty points they receive in-app to obtain discounts in-store. Customers can also use loyalty points to fund charitable programmes, such as the coronavirus pandemic and Ukraine crisis.

The creation of an app was the first step in an ambitious vision. Tomasz believes the app is an integral part of a broader ecosystem serving different aspects of a customer's lifestyle. For example, consumers can schedule online shopping

"Only hard work can bring results, regardless of intrinsic talent."

Tomasz Blicharski, Executive Vice President of the Management Board, Żabka Group

Scan code to watch the full interview.

pick-ups from local Żabka stores. They can also use the app to locate products that are approaching their expiry dates and take advantage of discounts.

Automating how people shop

Tomasz also helped his business roll out Żabka Nano autonomous convenience stores, such as those developed by Amazon Go in the US and UK. Today, Żabka has nearly 50 autonomous stores in Poland, which makes it the largest autonomous store chain in Europe. The stores operate in several formats such as standalone container-based vending machines, traditional brick-and-mortar, and store-within-a-store points of sale, each leveraging AI-powered computer vision technology created through close cooperation with American technology company AiFi. Tomasz says young people love the speed and freedom that autonomous shopping offers.

Żabka Nano stores are available to customers on a 24/7 basis. These AI-powered stores are well-suited to locations where convenience buying is attractive, such as near schools and offices. One of Żabka Nano stores in the capital city of Warsaw is testing Robbie, a hot-dog serving robot designed for Żabka. Tomasz says it is crucial to achieve a balance between humans and machines. He recognises many consumers still enjoy the social aspects of being served by a human though.

Finally, Tomasz and his team also recognised that younger people, although keen to eat healthy food, often have little time to shop. He introduced a direct-to-consumer service that customers can subscribe to and receive a daily delivery of healthy foods, covering breakfasts, snacks, and other meals. Maczfit service covers thousands of recipes and is very popular.

Creating a digital kitchen

With a dual agenda of optimising current operations and pushing new digital projects, Tomasz separated his teams into a traditional IT organisation that could produce fast and reliable outcomes, and a new digital team that could implement breakthrough concepts, such as autonomous stores. The latter team reported to a chief digital officer and provided translation between business requirements and technical solutions. Subsequently, Tomasz collapsed both organisations into a single unit. At the moment, about 15% of Żabka employees work on the company's digital development.

Tomasz likes to use the term technology rather than IT. He says the sole purpose of technology teams is to harness systems and services to deliver measurable business outcomes. He was a part of the team that introduced Agile methods to accelerate the pace of delivery and included all parties, from internal businesses to external franchisees, in the creation of minimum viable products. Tomasz is an enthusiast of digital platforms, such as Salesforce, to achieve scale and support stretched business goals.

Today, the technology group is divided into store products development, core process, infrastructure, security, governance team, product management team, and operations.

Defining the qualities of a Master Chef

Tomasz believes his secret sauce for effective leadership includes three ingredients:

- Creating a vision for the entire organisation including the autonomous stores
- Removing blockers and boundaries to give staff full freedom of access to resources
- Aligning business goals and rewards with all parties, including investors, staff, and external partners, such as franchisees

Tomasz believes only hard work can bring results, regardless of intrinsic talent. He says constant change is certain and advocates a growth mindset that encourages aspiring leaders to rely on the efforts of people around them.encourages aspiring leaders to rely on the efforts of people around them.

Verde gazpacho

Serves 2 portions

- 100g yellow tomatoes
- 1 cucumber, deseeded and cut into chunks
- 3 spring onions, chopped
- 1 small green chilli, deseeded and roughly chopped
- 1 small green pepper, deseeded and quartered
- 2 sticks celery, roughly chopped
- 1 clove garlic, peeled
- 200g baby spinach
- 30g fresh basil leaves
- 10g fresh parsley
- 10g fresh coriander
- 150g pine nuts
- 2 Tbsp sherry vinegar
- 3 Tbsp extra-virgin olive oil (ideally, use a peppery green oil)
- 50g baby watercress, saving a few leaves to garnish
- 500ml vegetable stock, cold
- 2 tsp sea salt flakes
- 2 tsp of freshly ground white pepper

For the croutons:

- 2 tsp sea salt flakes
- 3 Tbsp extra-virgin olive oil
- 2 thick slices of sourdough or farmhouse bread

The favourite dish of Javier Cabrerizo

This unique and flavoursome green Gazpacho recipe is a cold soup made from raw and freshly blended vegetables. It originated in the southern regions of the Iberian Peninsula. It is a popular soup widely enjoyed in Spain and Portugal, particularly during hot summers since it is usually served chilled (but not iced). Its crisp taste both refreshes and hydrates the palate and is packed with vitamins and minerals for those who are sick or hungover.

For the croutons, preheat the oven to 375°F / 190°C / Gas 5 and line a tray with baking sheet. Cut the sourdough or your favourite farmhouse bread into 1-inch (2-centimeter) cubes and toss with the olive oil and a bit of sea salt flakes. Spread the bread cubes evenly on the pan and bake it for about 10 minutes, or until the croutons turn golden and crisp. Remove from the oven and allow to cool down.

Roughly chop and mix all the ingredients and then blend them together in a food processor. Pour the mixture through a sieve to get rid of any lumps. Ideally, chill the soup for at least 2–3 hours or even better overnight for the taste to fully develop. Season with salt and pepper if needed.

To serve, pour the chilled gazpacho into 2 serving bowls, sprinkle over the crisp crotons and watercress leaves, then drizzle with more olive oil and sprinkle with sea salt flakes. Then, slurp away!

PLAYBOOK 1

MASTER CHEFS OF THE DIGITAL KITCHEN

Five characteristics that define successful CIOs

Great IT leadership is more important than ever. As the pace of digital transformation continues to quicken, the best CIOs rely on five key characteristics that help them turn the threat of disruption into an opportunity. They use these traits to lead the creation of new technology-enabled business models that generate a lasting competitive advantage.

That was one of the key findings that emerged from the first CIONET Cookbook in 2021, which highlighted how Master Chefs—who we define as the very best of European IT leadership—are more than leaders of their own domains. As well as leading agile and adept technology organisations, these Master Chefs create the conditions for a Digital Kitchen. Quite unlike the IT environment that dominated before, this outward-facing department exposes its methods to the diners who relish its first-class experiences.

Our analysis suggests Master Chefs of the Digital Kitchen excel across five traits: They are curious, imaginative, purposeful, authentic, and dynamic.

These five traits are distinct in nature, yet they interlink when it comes to leadership style. Master Chefs display all these traits, but they adopt and adapt them in a way that creates great results for them as individuals, and for the people they lead, the businesses they work for, and the customers they serve.

1. CURIOUS

The best digital leaders stimulate business innovation in a timely fashion

The best CIOs have a passion for everything that's new. Master Chefs search for weak signals constantly, whether that's emerging technologies or fresh business trends. As Group CIO at Tate & Lyle Sanjay Patel suggests, curiosity is an essential trait for effective digital leadership.

Curiosity isn't a solo activity. Successful CIOs engage closely with people and parties across and beyond the IT department. They explore and research weak signals internally and externally with colleagues and customers. By spotting these signals quickly and then testing their strength, CIOs stimulate business innovation in a timely fashion.

Master Chefs focus their attention on the user experience, whether that's in terms of the end customer or the employee. They work with line-of-business managers to deliver superior products and services that meet customer demands.

Great CIOs exploit information. They use data to elucidate trends and inform decision-making processes. They also use data analytics and artificial intelligence to personalise customer experiences across channels.

Master Chefs are always cooking up new ideas—and the best CIOs are rewarded for their curiosity. Digital leaders who build credibility are equal partners at the boardroom table. In fact, successful CIOs are often asked to take responsibility for other activities, such as procurement, supply chain, and risk management.

2. IMAGINATIVE

The best digital leaders are open-minded to diverse perspectives from anywhere

Long gone are the days when an IT leader was defined by their ability to keep technology systems up and running. The best CIOs look far beyond the enterprise firewall and are open-minded to diverse perspectives across an ecosystem of peers and partners.

IT can accelerate business innovation by providing new tools, digital platforms, and skills. In fact, the imaginative use of innovation can involve entire shifts in business models. It might also involve the more tactical use of imagination, like the creation of a dedicated innovation unit within an existing business such as Swiss Re, or the use of hackathons.

Erwin Verstraelen, CDIO at the Port of Antwerp, says the creation of an innovative culture is not a one-time task. Imaginative CIOs enable experimentation continually. Master Chefs who foster a culture of innovation focus on the funding, expertise, and capabilities for success.

Continual experimentation takes on many forms, yet imagination always relies on openness. Red Hat CDO Margaret Dawson fosters an open culture that encourages collaboration across organisational silos. Koen Vermeulen, Group CIO at Orange Group, uses open sourcing and processes to support a culture of collaboration.

One thing is certain: Ongoing digital transformation means the pressure is on CIOs to evaluate emerging technologies quickly. Corporate survival will depend on imaginative interventions to embrace these advances and fend off newcomers.

3. PURPOSEFUL

The best digital leaders ensure corporate cultures align with the emerging digital world

Organisational culture is one of the most important factors separating successful digital transformations from unsuccessful ones. The traditional IT structures and methods of the past are not fit for the fast-developing business requirements of tomorrow.

The watchword is purpose: Master Chefs identify clear business outcomes and create a purposeful

IT organisation where they, their teams, and their ecosystem partners understand what needs to be achieved. Reaching these targets is satisfying for the team and sustainable for the environment.

David Jack, formerly CTO at Dunnhumby, says top-down intervention is not the best way to orchestrate change. Instead, CIOs need teams of trusted experts who have autonomy, creative licence, and accountability for delivering change. Smart CIOs enable this shift through automation: let machines do the repetitive work, while employees focus on high-value activities.

Perhaps the most visible development in modern IT practices is to employ Agile. By applying lean thinking and Agile methods, such as short sprints, Master Chefs are baking success into the digital projects they undertake on behalf of the business.

What's clear is that purposeful CIOs develop a strong internal culture. Master Chefs foster organisational approaches to diversity, inclusivity, flexibility, and sustainability that extend across individual characteristics, values, beliefs, and backgrounds to ensure corporate cultures align with the emerging digital world.

4. AUTHENTIC

The best Master Chefs lead successfully by encouraging and inspiring others

When new challenges arise, people within the IT department and across other lines of business look to great CIOs for guidance. People trust these leaders to make the right decisions because they're authentic, and their passion for their role shines through.

Crucially, authentic leaders don't dictate the direction of travel. The best CIOs show humility. They lead by encouraging and inspiring others, working across silos to eliminate blockers to change. Master Chefs use terms like conductor, orchestrator, and connector to describe this proactive approach.

Master Chefs also recognise the importance of communication. The right language is crucial to gaining influence within an organisation. Yes, digital transformation is often about implementing technology, but the board is interested in outcomes, not bits and bytes.

Successful CIOs explain digital transformation in terms the rest of the business understands. When people know what you're saying, they think of you as an authentic leader. So, instead of talking about technology stacks, Kensington Mortgages COO Mark Foulsham focuses on business terms, such as earnings and customer impact.

Master Chefs celebrate their success and use storytelling to engage the organisation, but they do so in a way that shows how the actions they pursue are best for the company, rather than the CIO as an individual. They are, in short, always authentic.

5. DYNAMIC

The best digital leaders adjust rapidly to fast-changing circumstances

If change is now the overriding constant in business, whether that's responding to crises, adopting digital services, or switching business models, then adopting flexible business structures based on open sourcing and Agile development methods is key.

CIOs who break free from the old world of legacy systems and waterfall techniques create the dynamic IT department that a modern business requires. Instead of a proliferation of data silos, Master Chefs bring services together on modern, cloud-based platforms. They help the business procure its own solutions safely and securely.

Effective CIOs work with external partners tactically to develop flexible platforms for change, while internal teams focus on strategic issues that generate value. An example: open-source standards and scalable cloud platforms have enabled Dunnhumby's 3,000 staff to employ common tools and share vital data resources.

New challenges continue to emerge. Cindy Hoots, CDO and CIO at AstraZeneca, says her team supported the development of the coronavirus vaccine. Automation tools, such as robotic process automation (RPA) and artificial intelligence (AI), helped human talent meet stretched goals.

Incredible results in extreme circumstances show the value of a dynamic approach. CIOs must love the problem, not the solution. Technology is simply the conduit to reaching business objectives—and the more flexible the platforms, the better for all concerned.

New challenges bring new opportunities

The best CIOs aren't just experts within their own domain; they are capable business leaders who help their organisations embrace the myriad of challenges that define the modern world. Master Chefs go above and beyond the technology department. These leaders possess characteristics that help them change their businesses for the better.

Yet there's good news for IT leaders who feel they're not ready to reach the heights of the Master Chefs—you too can create a high-quality Digital Kitchen. As Ministry of Defence CIO Charlie Forte makes clear, with persistence and patience, any leader can transform an organisation successfully.

As we show in this year's CIONET Cookbook, CIOs have fresh opportunities to bring the best offerings from their Digital Kitchen to the boardroom table. Now is the time to be a Master Chef and help the business apply technology to deliver new competitive advantages.

PLAYBOOK 2

REIMAGINING WORK

The world of work has changed fundamentally, and CIOs must help their organisations build a digital workforce that's fit for future challenges

The old way of working is gone forever. The coronavirus pandemic triggered the largest shift in working practices in modern times. The shift will not be temporary: CIONET research suggests this disruption is likely to persist. We must now think carefully about the role that intelligent automation and digital talent play in helping corporations adapt to the new normal.

Fundamental change, now and forever

The past two years have seen a fundamental technological and socio-economic transformation. From the outbreak of the pandemic to the adoption of video-conferencing technology and onto the emergence of hybrid working, there has been a reimagining of work. So, what do these fundamental transformations mean for the business and its leaders? Here's what we believe are the change imperatives facing the C-suite across the three core areas of workflow, workforce, and workplace:

Workflow: Boards will shift their focus from operational excellence to customer experience. Making this shift is the only way that boards can hope to compete with the rising tide of digital-native businesses that found new ways to flourish during the pandemic. The shift to customer experience necessitates cutting out large swathes of internal projects that concentrate on modernising the factory. Instead, business leaders should apply their scarce investment resources to enhancing all stages of the customer journey, from product or service acquisition through to lifecycle management.

Workforce: Traditional pools of localised labour will need to be supplemented by global as well as digital talent. The pandemic has demonstrated that staff can work successfully away from the office—and this realisation is likely to mean employees spend much less time in the corporate headquarters in the future. This shift to remote working is likely to sponsor far greater fluidity in the sourcing of professional and managerial staff. Commensurate advances in artificial intelligence (AI) and machine learning (ML), or what we refer to as digital talent, will absorb many of the routine elements of day-to-day work.

Workplace: Organisations will need to reduce their office footprint by between 30% and 50% over time, casting off regimental rows of screen-based workers in favour of creative spaces that encourage team-based working—what we describe as heads-up and heads-together working. Heads-down working will be largely confined to the home or less costly satellite offices. The office of the future will have an emphasis on social and flexible meeting spaces. Blue-chip enterprises will adopt these arrangements to encourage staff to spend their time in the office socially and productively.

Across workflow, workforce, and workplace, we believe the combination of these concurrent changes will enable organisations to become more agile through the adoption of the following approaches:

- An asset-lite approach to property, infrastructure, and human resources, reducing fixed costs and increasing operational flexibility
- A digital workforce, combining humans and digital talent that will be more innovative by responding creatively to external changes
- End-to-end workflow automation that will accelerate operational agility and draw trading partners into a close-knit ecosystem

The result of this transformation in working practices could be a virtuous circle that places innovation at the top of the corporate agenda.

Understanding the potential blockers

Our discussions with digital leaders have exposed barriers to a transformation in working practices. We believe many of these blockers can be overcome by adopting intelligent automation, which is the use of technology to support partially skilled digital workers. Potential barriers to transformation include:

- Legacy debt that encompasses outdated systems, processes, and infrastructures that are too costly to replace. Intelligent automation can help to integrate legacy and modern systems by removing cumbersome manual interfaces.
- Fragmented data that coalesces to create a vast pool of unexploited resources. Intelligent automation can help organisations clean data and codify knowledge, helping companies to develop deeper insights and tap into new sources of value.
- Legacy skills and cultures that resist change. The move to a digital workforce can help boost perceptions of work by removing repetition and creating a focus on creativity. This change should motivate employees, especially the incoming, digital-savvy generation.

The big pay-off from the introduction of intelligent automation could be the development of Knowledge as a Service (KaaS) techniques that help to capture, codify, and apply the abundant expertise that is currently locked in the minds of employees. This development could lead to the birth of new technologies and specialists, similar to what happened with

Software as a Service (SaaS) and the emergence of major players like Salesforce and Workday.

Developing a roadmap towards a digital workforce

The past two years have provided a once-in-a-lifetime opportunity to rethink how we do business. We believe this process should now focus on how we organise work according to our three core dimensions: workflow, workforce, and workplace. For digital leaders and their C-suite peers, we believe the practical implications across our three core areas will be as follows:

Workflow

1. Do fewer things: Prioritise, don't optimise. All workflow enhancements should put customers at the core of the business and reinforce the importance of their journey. Intelligent automation can help to enrich and increase the speed of customer interactions, while also boosting the relevance of business responses to client enquiries.
2. Do things differently: Organisations should focus on the end-to-end automation of critical workflows to create a connected company that operates seamlessly across functional silos. This integration will help to improve agility and flexibility. Intelligent automation can also help to integrate separate applications that are embedded within complex processes.
3. Do different things: Examine workflows to identity areas in which knowledge can be mapped and codified to provide new revenue sources, such as KaaS. Digital talent can help capture and codify knowledge from individual workers, providing a universal knowledge base across an organisation and out to its external parties.

Workforce

4. Do fewer things: There is still much potential to automate repetitive tasks and to improve interfaces between humans and machines. Intelligent automation can help relieve humans of many mundane but necessary tasks, leaving them to concentrate on higher-value activities.
5. Do things differently: Augmentation of more complex professional tasks will become a practical possibility with advances in AI and ML. Managers and professional workers will depend on robots to support decision-making processes.
6. Do different things: The nature of work itself will need to be redefined as digital assets begin to enter the workplace in large num bers. Equality between human and digital talent could help to transform the structures of current organisations to make them more agile and responsive.

Workspace

1. Do fewer things: Security has become a key issue. Employees are mixing devices and applications for work and pleasure. Nefarious cyber activity has looked to exploit this overlap. Intelligent automation can strengthen security and improve identification and authentication processes.
2. Do things differently: Enterprises have invested in asset-heavy infrastructures, such as centre-city offices. There was little encouragement to work from home previously, but this sentiment has changed dramatically since March 2020. The move to remote working is encouraging executives to consider an asset-lite approach to physical buildings.
3. Do different things: Hybrid working is likely to reduce overall social interaction. However, staff will continue to value the social aspects of work, so executives should turn their attention to workspaces that are designed to foster creativity and collaboration.

Implications for IT leaders

To make a successful transition to a full-fledged digital business, boards will need to address legacy cultures, processes, and skills. Our research suggests that cultures and skills will be the primary challenges compared to technical issues. In this respect, preparing for a digital workforce will require a great deal of planning and communication.

The message for IT leaders is clear: Become business advisers and partners rather than technical operators. The day-to-day choice of IT systems and vendors is rapidly devolving to functions and lines of business. IT leaders need to focus on business opportunities that are technology-enabled, as well as strengthening enterprise architectures to improve governance and consistency.

The CIO should be a genuine business partner, acting as a consultant to the lines of business. This role will require a practical grasp of new-wave technologies, such as intelligent automation, and a sensitivity to the weak signals emerging on the horizon. However, CIOs should also devote time to automating IT services, so they and their teams can concentrate on business priorities. It is here we believe intelligent automation and digital talent present an opportunity to transform the speed and quality of IT services.

In conclusion, future success will be linked directly to a closer collaboration between business and IT leaders, with both sharing common objectives. The pandemic highlighted deficiencies in incumbent structures and processes when compared to digital natives. This gap must be closed if incumbents are to survive and flourish in the decade ahead. The move to a digital workforce should become a top priority at board levels if incumbents are to achieve the agility and speed of their digital competitors.

Quesa-mosa

Serves 2 portions

Samosa Filling

- 480g or 2 large potatoes, boiled & cubed
- 75g peas, boiled and lightly mashed
- 3 tsp coriander leaves, finely chopped
- 1 green or red chilli, finely chopped
- 1 tsp cumin seeds
- 2 tsp ginger, shredded or powder
- 1 pinch asafoetida (hing)
- 1 tsp garam masala
- 1 tsp amchur (mango powder)
- 2 Tbsp oil or ghee
- 1 tsp lemon juice

Quesa-mosa is an innovative Indian-Mexican fusion starter made up of yummy samosa filling and lip-smacking tangy sweet tomato chutney (an alternative play on salsa), all tucked nicely and covered over with melted cheese in a quesadilla. This easy to assemble recipe cleverly combines two all-time favourites of Indian and Mexican cuisine and amalgamates it all into one wonderfully scrumptious dish.

To prepare the samosa filling, heat ghee or oil in pan on medium heat. Add cumin seeds to "awaken" the spices. Once the cumin seeds begin to splutter, add hing, ginger, and garlic and let them sizzle in the oil for a minute. Add diced potatoes and peas and the rest of the spices except lemon juice. Stir and cook for about 3–4 minutes until they are all nicely mingled and heated throughout. Turn the gas off and mix in lemon juice. The samosa filling is now ready.

For the tasty tomato chutney, bring a pan of water to a low simmer. Score the bottom of the tomatoes with a knife and heat the tomatoes on a low simmer for 5 minutes. Drain the tomatoes and allow to cool, then peel the skins and dice the tomatoes. Using a sauté pan, add the oil over medium heat and proceed to add the cumin, mustard powder, turmeric, chili powder, chilis and garlic. Cook for 1 minute. Stir in the tomatoes, salt, sugar, and bay leaf. Cover and simmer for 10 minutes. Remove the lid and simmer for 5 more minutes until chunky and thickened.

Now to assemble this chef-d'oeuvre, heat a tortilla on stove in a non-stick pan. Spread a thick lavish layer of the tomato chutneys on the tortilla. Then add a heaping portion of the samosa filling, oodles of cheddar cheese and crumble some tortilla chips over the top for a crunchy bite. Fold in half and then quarter (so it looks like a samosa) and cook on medium heat until browned, then flip and cook on other side, ensuring all the glorious cheese is melted. Hola & Gracias!

The favourite dish of Kristin Lindmark

Tomato Chutney

- 8 tomatoes
- 2 tsp vegetable oil
- 2 green chillies, seeds removed, finely chopped
- 1 tsp cumin
- 1 tsp mustard powder
- ½ tsp turmeric
- 1 tsp mild chili powder
- 2 garlic cloves, finely chopped or grated
- ¼ tsp salt
- ½ tsp granulated sugar
- 1 bay leaf

Quesadilla

- 8 Tortilla
- 3 cups cheddar cheese, shredded
- Tortilla chips, optional for crunch

SECTION 2
DESIGNING TASTY RECIPES

★★★★★

"Corporate complacency is unacceptable; today's businesses must help their employees adapt to fast-changing circumstances."

Europe has witnessed sluggish economic growth and near flatlining productivity during the past two decades. Private companies have barely grown their revenues ahead of the Retail Price Index. Public services continue to bloat, absorbing an ever-increasing share of economic resources. This stagnation has occurred despite trillions of dollars of technology-driven investment. In sharp contrast, Big Tech giants, such as Amazon, Apple, Google, Meta, and Microsoft, have achieved double-digit growth rates. Today, these five companies have a higher value than all the European stock markets put together.

What emerges, in short, is a tale of sharply contrasting fortunes. Against this backdrop, a cadre of determined digital leaders are looking to use digital and data processes to help their businesses grow. This section explores the recipes of these Master Chefs, showcasing how these pioneers are leading digital transformation programmes at some of Europe's biggest organisations.

One message that comes through loud and clear is that corporate complacency is unacceptable. The easy availability of cheap money has come to an end, inflation has risen to double-digit figures and energy prices have soared. Perhaps the biggest mistake by IT leaders in recent years has been to direct huge amounts of investment into monolithic ERP platforms, such as SAP and Oracle. This focus has deflected attention away from the end customer and perpetuated rigid structures that are inflexible to new requirements.

Today's businesses must help their employees adapt to fast-changing circumstances. Master Chefs from DB Schenker, Euroclear, and Carl Zeiss provide powerful illustrations of how modern approaches to automation, such as robotic process automation (RPA) and artificial intelligence (AI), can help streamline back-office processes. These approaches can eliminate menial tasks while enhancing customer experiences, accelerating product developments, and simplifying external interactions. Our first playbook "Towards the Fully Automated Enterprise" describes how RPA and AI are being used to boost productivity through broader staff empowerment. Here, Master Chefs set direction, provide the tools, and then allow their workers to get on with their jobs.

Our second playbook, entitled "The Data Playbook for Wine Connoisseurs," explores how the deployment of a data-centric business model can transform the speed and effectiveness of decision-making processes at every level of the organisation. We believe data centricity is a prerequisite for growth and productivity improvements. The deployment of data-centric business models is no easy task. However, there is an effective path forward. Master Chefs from HEINEKEN® and GNV demonstrate how a combination of modern tools, flexible platforms and staff empowerment can operationalise visionary strategies that unleash the true potential of the organisation.

Master Chefs at Prosegur and Red Hat conclude the section by addressing the biggest challenge of all: how to deliver genuine business innovation. The scale of this challenge is manifest in our playbook "Closing the Innovation Gap," with one chief executive at a telecommunications firm stating that "innovation is our lifeblood, but we still cannot innovate." Prosegur's Master Chef cuts through organisational inertia by separating the core business from new software-driven operations. Red Hat's Master Chef, meanwhile, advocates for the adoption of open-source techniques that help to standardise commodity activities within the core, while opening the door for innovation at the periphery.

A common theme running through the recipes in this section is the need to replace rigid and monolithic technology platforms with adaptive structures that take advantage of cloud platforms, software services and open-source standards. In an age of uncertainty and almost constant change, modern IT underpinnings are a prerequisite for end-to-end process transformation that can deliver much needed revenue growth and productivity improvements.

THREE
AUTOMATION

Despite trillions of Euros of investment in IT during the past two decades, productivity across Europe remains disappointingly flat. To escape the prevailing situation, the Master Chefs in this section recognise they will need to adopt radical approaches to deal with a combination of factors, including rising customer expectations, hybrid working and supply chain disruption.

The three recipes in this subsection highlight how modern automation techniques are being applied by DB Schenker—a global logistics company—Euroclear, and Carl Zeiss. Each recipe provides unique insights into why automation is so necessary today; where it is most effective in delivering business value, and how it can be deployed rapidly to improve productivity.

In terms of why automation is necessary, it is clear that the coronavirus pandemic led to a step change in processes. Most commercial transactions in the post-pandemic age now take place online—and supply chains are stretched to their limits. Digital natives have proven themselves to be adept in this new environment, casting a shadow over their competitors.

When it comes considering where and how automation is necessary, the focus of IT in all three recipes has moved from streamlining back-office operations to enhancing customer experiences. Automation is helping Euroclear speed up new service offerings by providing all parties with one view of the development process. Zeiss is using machine vision, AI, and RPA to accelerate product innovation. At DB Schenker, automation is helping to eliminate 30% of back-office tasks.

The Master Chefs in this subsection recognise that a top-down approach has limitations. Only by empowering every individual within the organisation can automation take root effectively and deliver tangible outcomes.

DB Schenker

Automating to compete successfully

Ingredients

- The full potential of automation in every aspect of a global logistics business must be appreciated and go hand in hand with the passion to make change happen
- The roles and responsibilities of the CFO and CIO need to be viewed as complementary, to ensure they contribute jointly to successful outcomes
- The big picture and vision must be fully communicated to bring every member of the team together in a self-organising IT unit

Preparing the dish

Christa Koenen is CIO and CDO at DB Schenker, one of the world's leading logistics companies. She is a board member with career experiences span marketing, finance, and technology. Her IT&D organisation's staff is spread across the Americas, Europe, Middle East Africa, and Asia. As a Master Chef, Christa displays the vision and passion to keep DB Schenker at the forefront of digital innovation and growth.

DB Schenker is a division of German rail operator Deutsche Bahn. The company was acquired by Deutsche Bahn as Schenker-Stinnes in 2002. The business comprises divisions for air, land, sea freight, and contract logistics, employing more than 75,000 staff.

Positioning automation as a top business priority

The last few years have been rewarding for companies that adapt to fast-changing customer needs. The potential rewards are high in logistics, where there has

"A healthy tension between finance and technology leads to beneficial outcomes."

Christa Koenen, CIO and CDO, DB Schenker

been a radical change in demand due to the coronavirus pandemic, supply chain disruptions and digital transformation. Christa believes her ability to lead change is her secret ingredient as a successful CIO. She says automation has a central role to play by lowering costs and diverting human resources to value-adding activities.

DB Schenker employees deal with a wide variety of user interfaces and "mountains of paper." Manual processing can be expensive and inaccurate. Automation of the customer interface using robotic process automation and artificial intelligence helps improve quality and build customer trust. DB Schenker has generated 150+ use cases at the front end of the business. It has introduced the intelligent chatbot Betty to automate routine inquiries across eight European countries.

Christa is now extending automation into production areas, such as the warehouse. She believes autonomous vehicles are the next step in supply chain automation and applies new techniques, including sensors, to help track parcels and vehicle movements. In back-office functions, such as finance and procurement, Christa believes automation could displace more than 30% of labour. Automation can eliminate mundane tasks and release human talent to focus on creative activities. The main challenge now is to scale-up automation capabilities across all regions and business units. IT relies on its internal business customers to identify pain points and request automated solutions.

Group IT has established a centre of excellence to provide automation guidelines and tools globally. Christa encourages technology leaders at the regional and business-unit levels to drive automation using these guidelines and tools. She says there's never enough expertise at the core to cover all requirements, so priorities can be shaped at regional and local levels.

Allocating responsibilities for automation

Having been a CFO prior to her current CIO/CDO role, Christa understands how finance can help to accelerate automation. Both roles have a comprehensive overview of the business. Christa says a healthy tension between finance and technology leads to beneficial outcomes. The CFO focuses on cost and stability, whereas the CIO brings new ideas that can lead to business innovation.

Christa believes in full transparency between finance and IT. A decade ago, IT was seen by its peers as complex and mysterious. The CIO had a monopoly on all-things

Scan code to watch the full interview.

technical. Today, most C-level executives have a stronger awareness of technology. IT is being emancipated across business boundaries. Citizen development tools such as low code/no code bring further democratisation.

Organising IT for success

Christa has adopted a matrix structure within her global IT&D function. She has a team at head office that focuses on infrastructure and governance. Regional CIOs and business IT leads work closely with their local peers to implement new solutions, including automation.

As a 150-year-old business, DB Schenker has heritage systems that must be replaced. Many large systems have already been modernised and moved to cloud platforms, such as transport management systems. IT is now focusing on further applications. DB Schenker has adopted Agile development techniques to accelerate modernisation, using mixed technical and business teams.

Christa's main challenge is to find the best resources to manage an avalanche of change. She believes logistics is an attractive area for modern IT, digital, and business professionals. Within IT&D, the wide spectrum of tasks between legacy modernisation and technological innovation provides an enticing menu.

Defining the qualities of a Master Chef

Christa says Master Chefs paint the big picture and communicate its finer details to every member of staff. She is keen to share commercial information where possible, so that staff understand how they fit into the big picture. This approach has enabled Christa to transform a traditional, hierarchical management structure into a self-organising unit in her prior role. She believes bottom-up change is only possible when every member of staff is self-activated.

Christa is keen to see DB Schenker make changes for the better, whether to increase customer satisfaction, generate revenue growth, or contribute to sustainability. She works hard to ensure every employee takes responsibility to produce benefits. As a change agent, she recognises the need to inspire, but also to be patient and hold back to allow people to catch up with her vision. Christa asks her staff to explain technical solutions to her in easy-to-understand terms, which encourages IT experts to think carefully about the potential benefits of any new technology.

One of Christa's personal advantages has been to work in several different countries during her career. She has gathered a wider set of ingredients as a Master Chef, both cultural and technical, and applies these to complex business problems. While she believes automation can help overcome many business challenges, she warns against over-automating. People have an ever-more valuable role within the digital economy. Training and confidence will help them rise to this opportunity.

Euroclear

Harnessing the Force to deliver digital transformation

Ingredients

- Euroclear must become a software business if it is to respond effectively to changes in capital markets
- Close collaboration with the business will bring improved results, as Agile techniques are applied to new "offer development" at the concept, design, and production stages
- A comprehensive transformation of the workplace, workforce, and workflows must be undertaken to achieve sustainable change

Preparing the dish

Michal Paprocki is the Group CTO and Joint CIO of Euroclear. Having started his professional career as an economist with both a degree and MBA, he joined ING Bank, spending 16 years in IT and operations. In 2018 Michal moved to Euroclear, which involved a change in industry, country, and work environment. Being charged with helping to transform Euroclear into a software company made the role an appealing challenge.

Euroclear is a Belgium-based financial services company that specialises in the settlement of securities transactions, as well as the safekeeping and asset servicing of these securities. The company was founded in 1968 to help settle trades on the fast-developing Eurobonds market. Today, Euroclear serves 2,000 financial institutions and offers settlement and asset deposits for equities, bonds, derivatives, and other financial instruments. The company is responsible for $36 trillion of settlements each year.

Wising up to potential market disruptions

Euroclear is under pressure to adapt its well-proven network model because of a combination of cost pressures, regulatory requirements, and new customer expectations across the globe. Michal also recognises that fast-moving FinTech companies could exploit new techniques such as blockchain to attempt to undermine Euroclear's business-leading position.

The response to these challenges has been coloured by optimism. Euroclear has reinvented itself multiple times during its 50-plus years of operations. Michal recognises that settlement and deposit activities will become commoditised, but the entry price to compete is high. Euroclear will continue to be successful if it leverages the data that is generated by the trillions of transactions that pass through its network.

Euroclear is adopting both an offensive and defensive strategy to deal with changing market conditions. Securities can be used as collateral, which helps to reduce market risk and generate new sources of insight and revenue. Knowing your customer is often the best form of defence, providing data insights across the entire value chain.

Undertaking digital transformation

Almost half of Euroclear's staff are IT professionals. Transforming the core business has required a more intensive dialogue between IT and the business. The IT organisation has helped to set the pace of change by achieving greater velocity within its own activities. The steps taken by Michal include shrinking development cycles, in-sourcing key activities, and adopting an open architecture.

Instead of waiting for the commercial function to handover new product designs in a sequential fashion, the IT team now works with the business to co-develop new offerings from inception to market launch. This joined-up approach allows Euroclear to respond rapidly to its customers' needs. The company can place bigger bets by validating each incremental development and undertaking quarterly financial reviews to manage internal risk closely. Michal has placed Agile development processes at the heart of this transformation. Euroclear delivers over a third of all projects through Agile already and has plans to accelerate adoption further.

Reinventing work, reinventing business

Any major reinvention of Euroclear needs to cover at least three

"Pass on what you have learned."

Michal Paprocki, Group CTO, Euroclear

Scan code to watch the full interview.

dimensions beyond technology: workplace, workforce, and workflow. Michal has been involved in bringing change across these three areas due to his influential position within the business.

Before the coronavirus pandemic, Euroclear insisted on all staff working from its offices. In early 2020, staff were reassigned to home working and the company benefited from an early decision to roll out Microsoft Teams. Today, most staff spend three days working from home. Michal sees the office as a creative space where staff can spend two days a week working with colleagues. The extensive use of Agile techniques means the company needs room to accommodate white boards and relaxation areas.

Euroclear is also changing its workforce and moving away from a talent-sourcing approach that has traditionally focused on functional skills. As Agile becomes common practice, the organisation needs fewer, more qualified, and digitally savvy staff who can work across functional silos. It's always challenging to acquire such talented staff, especially when you're in competition with FinTechs. Michal says Euroclear offers a respected and friendly place to work, where IT employees can impact business outcomes. He looks for workers with curiosity, adaptability, and diversity.

Finally, Michal is also helping to transform workflow at Euroclear. The company has started to automate existing paper-based processes by implementing robotic process automation. RPA has helped remove discrepancies from back-office workflows and is helping the business handle multiple tax residencies. RPA is also helping tackle money laundering by analysing issuer provenance. Across all areas of influence, RPA can be redesigned or reinvented as requirements change, which is an essential element in a move to a software-based organisation.

Defining the qualities of a Master Chef

Michal draws an analogy between his game-changing role as a CTO and a Jedi Knight in the film Star Wars. Michal believes effective leadership is about using wisdom and patience to bring the workforce with you. The transformational tasks that Michal is responsible for involve injecting energy and technology into every part of the organisation, which he calls "the Force." He must concentrate on closing the gap between vision and reality.

Michal is helping to lead a transformational journey at Euroclear that is taking the company from a traditional, hierarchical organisation into a world of employee empowerment. Michal achieves success by exploiting servant leadership, where his key function is to nurture teams and help people grow. This role is analogous to being a shepherd, where he always tries to listen more and talk less. To quote Jedi Master Yoda: "Pass on what you have learned."

Carl Zeiss AG

Being successful by doing the things you love

Ingredients

- A corporate purpose built around social values gives strength to every employee across the globe
- A high-tech company that embraces new techniques enables you to stay ahead of your competition
- Work/life balance and an empowered staff that loves what they do bring success

Preparing the dish

Carsten Trapp is Group CIO of Carl Zeiss AG. Having become hooked on computing during childhood, he has pursued his passion for IT throughout his career, starting in the pharmaceutical sector with Merck Group and entering Zeiss in 2017 in the medical and life sciences division. In 2020, he was appointed Group CIO, where he is responsible for IT across all Carl Zeiss businesses.

Carl Zeiss is owned by the Foundation Carl Zeiss Stiftung and manufactures optical systems and opto-electronics, with 35,000 employees. Founded in 1846, the company now operates a multinational business in 50 countries, with 30 production sites and around 25 development sites.

Despite its size and global distribution, Zeiss is driven by a sense of purpose around technology enablement in critical areas, such as patient care and the production of silicon chips that support a new era of hyper-connectivity and hyper-personalisation. Technology is a key element in helping the company lead in vital areas of healthcare and commerce.

"Successful CIOs and their teams deliver on their promises."

Carsten Trapp, Group CIO, Carl Zeiss AG

Scan code to watch the full interview.

Maintaining a position of power

Carsten says three change drivers are important when it comes to the ability of Zeiss to maintain leadership in its sector: technology, regulations, and customer requirements.

He says embracing technology trends early helps the company deploy the best techniques ahead of the competition. Zeiss has adopted a proactive strategy that meticulously assesses technical developments, such as artificial intelligence. Investment is focused on the areas with the greatest potential for a commercial and societal impact.

Zeiss recognises the constant threat of cyberattacks and the need for effective information security. The company pays close attention to industry regulations. Carsten says this approach means "doing things right," which includes thorough documentation of all technology-led projects to ensure compliance. This concentration on regulation and documentation makes it much easier to undertake audits as part of the daily business routine.

Finally, the company uses technology to simplify and streamline customer interfaces. Carsten draws a comparison with the automotive sector, where technology has been introduced across the end-to-end supply chain to help boost responsiveness to customer requirements.

Sustaining industrial leadership

A range of technical developments have prompted Zeiss to restructure itself over its 175 years. Starting in 1847 with the production of optical microscopes, Zeiss diversified into cameras in 1861 and binoculars in 1964.

More recently, it invented extreme ultraviolet lithography to enable the production of semiconductor chips and has developed electron and ion microscopes to supersede optical technology. Carsten says these technical and structural innovations helped prepare Zeiss for the modern challenges the business faces.

Reorganising how the business works

As a technology company, Zeiss must employ flexible structures, modern employment practices, and digital workflows to develop innovative and reliable products and services for its customers.

Carsten recognises the profound impact of the recent pandemic on the way his staff works. He has equipped Zeiss with a modern infrastructure that combines video and audio connectivity to enable staff to work from anywhere.

Hybrid working has become the norm, with an expectation that employees will commute to the office for between 25% and 50% of the working week. The reduction in the number of staff in the office has created extra workspace that is being used to develop creative spaces. The offices are being redesigned to reflect new ways of working.

Zeiss has always cared about its employees. Today, the company recognises it is necessary to trust and empower its staff, no matter where they work. Diversity is also important when sourcing new skills. Adopting a global workforce has helped shift the firm's traditional culture from one based around Germany to a more universal mindset.

To help Zeiss stay competitive, Carsten is employing a range of digital tools, such as RPA, AI, machine learning, and machine vision. He recognises that IT professionals have talked about workforce automation for 20-plus years with little effect, yet he is optimistic that RPA provides a step change in the company's efforts to automate back- and front-office functions. Zeiss is also using AI and machine vision to assure quality in lens production. These technologies enhance human effectiveness in complex production environments.

Creating a digital powerhouse

Zeiss runs both a digital and an IT organisation, where the latter takes responsibility for infrastructure and core systems. While there can be grey zones between these separate functions, Carsten strives to ensure the departments work seamlessly together. IT is organised around a corporate centre and regional units. The governance principle that Carsten adopts is "one IT," which operates in accordance with the "one family" philosophy of the broader Zeiss group.

Traditionally, IT at Zeiss was heavily outsourced. The ever-increasing requirement to pilot and deploy technology at speed means Carsten strives to maintain key expertise in-house. However, the war for talent means he still depends on external parties to fill key gaps. Zeiss is adopting DevOps techniques in some areas of the business, but Carsten says this principle is not a universal solution.

Defining the qualities of a Master Chef

Carsten loves his work and expects his staff to share his passion for computing and digital technologies. He sees the role of the CIO as an orchestrator rather than an autocratic manager and seeks to empower his staff wherever possible.

Carsten believes that teams and their managers must be bold and make decisions. To be successful, there is no room for indifference. His core values align with many other digital leaders in this Cookbook and include honesty, reliability, and trust. Successful CIOs and their teams, says Carsten, deliver on their promises.

Normandy Chicken and Calvados Casserole

Serves 2

- 250–300g diced chicken thigh
- 4 Tbsp French unsalted butter
- 2 whole apples, cored and sliced
- 1 yellow sweet onion, sliced
- 50g soft cheese or heavy cream
- 20g or 1 Tbsp wholegrain mustard or Dijon Mustard
- 40g Calvados Apple Brandy or Apple Cider
- 300ml chicken stock
- 2 garlic cloves, minced
- 1 tsp dry thyme
- 5g chives
- 80g French beans
- 1 baguette or any bread you like
- Flour, olive oil, pepper, salt

This is a famous French chicken dish that originated in the northern France region of Normandy, which is known for its apples, apple cider, and brandy. This recipe is a much-loved autumn dish that is luxurious yet simple to make! This warming casserole combines diced chicken thighs, braised in apple cider or apple brandy, then cooked with onions, garlic, and herbs, and finally finished off in a rich, delectable, and creamy stew.

To start, preheat the oven to 220°C / 200°C (fan) / gas 7. Heat a large, wide-based, oven-proof casserole dish with a drizzle of olive oil over a medium-high heat. Cut the apples into wedges, removing the core but leaving the skin on. Peel and cut the sweet yellow onion into wedges. Add the diced chicken thighs to the dish, coating them with 1 tsp flour and cooking it for 30 seconds. Add the apple brandy or cider and cook for another 30 seconds, then proceed to add the chopped apples and onion wedges with the crushed garlic and thyme and give everything a good hearty stir. Add the chicken stock with 250ml boiled water, stirring in thoroughly the wholegrain/Dijon mustard and heavy cream or soft cheese. Bring everything to the boil over a high heat, then put the dish in the oven, uncovered, for 35–45 min or until the chicken is cooked through.

Once the casserole is almost ready, trim the French beans with a drizzle of olive oil and a pinch of sea salt. Add the baguette or your favourite bread to the other side of the tray and put the tray in the oven for 7–9 min or until the French beans are tender and the bread are warm and crusty.

To serve, chop the chives and sprinkle them all over the Normandy chicken and apple casserole, then season with pepper and salt. Serve the French beans and crusty baguettes alongside the casserole and Bon Appetit!

The favourite dish of Natasha Davydova

FOUR
DIGITAL TRANSFORMATION

The two recipes in this subsection illustrate how successful digital transformation is dependent on a compelling strategy combined with effective execution. HEINEKEN® has adopted what it refers to as an EverGreen strategy, which sets the course for radical transformation. GNV, an Italian shipping company, has seized on punctuality as the centrepiece for its digital business.

HEINEKEN®'s EverGreen strategy is driven by the business goal of achieving carbon neutrality by 2040. To achieve this outcome, HEINEKEN® is transforming itself into a digital business that combines global scale and scope with local market sensitivity. Key to this transformation is a unifying IT platform based on SAP's S/4HANA, supplemented by the tactical use of Software as a Service applications. This combination allows the firm to implement digital processes across the entire supply chain, from the extraction of raw materials to the production of goods for end customers.

For GNV, punctuality is the hallmark of a successful freight and passenger shipping company in today's competitive environment. Achieving high levels of punctuality can be a tough ask for any fleet operator in the face of rapidly changing external factors. GNV's solution to this challenge has been to adopt a data-first approach, which integrates external data sources with information from internal systems, and a network of embedded sensors within the shipping fleet.

Both Master Chefs emphasise the importance of a can-do attitude when leaders look to convert ambitious strategies into digital business models. In the words of the GNV Master Chef Barbara Poli: "If you can dream it, you can do it." The hard part, however, is mobilising an effective community that is inspired by change and overcoming internal barriers to demonstrate tangible outcomes.

HEINEKEN® N.V.

Thriving in a fast-changing world

Ingredients

- An EverGreen strategy to deliver superior and balanced growth provides the next evolution of the HEINEKEN® business
- Digital transformation will help identify the route to consumer whilst modernizing and simplifying the IT landscape globally

Preparing the dish

Breno Gentil is a senior director at HEINEKEN®, where he leads Digital and Technology across Europe. Born in Brazil to an engineering family, his father encouraged him to take up coding in early childhood. He studied Computer Engineering at university, did a master's in Design, and later an MBA. Reader's Digest was his first job after university, where he helped establish and grow its business in Brazil. This experience gave him the taste of working for a start-up, as he was only the fifth member of a national team that rapidly grew to more than 100. Prior to joining HEINEKEN® in 2022, Breno worked at Mondelez, then 15 years at British American Tobacco (BAT), rising to CTO for the Group.

HEINEKEN® was established in 1864 when Gerard Adriaan Heineken bought Amsterdam's Haystack brewery, which dated back to 1592. Today, HEINEKEN® comprises more than 300 brands and has become the world's most international brewer. The company prides itself in stretching its products into fresh areas, including non-alcoholic beers. This search for fresh ideas requires continuous innovation enhanced by digital capabilities. As a family company, HEINEKEN® is committed to business growth in a sustainable manner that generates long-term value for all its stakeholders.

"Our thoughts make up our lives."

Breno Gentil, Senior Director Digital & Technology Europe, HEINEKEN®

Scan code to watch the full interview.

Building an EverGreen strategy

Despite short-term pressures such as the pandemic, energy shortages, and inflation, HEINEKEN® has a bold business strategy known as EverGreen that reflects its long-term ambitions. The strategy has five priorities:

- Drive superior growth with greater focus on the needs of consumers and customers.
- Fund the growth by addressing the cost base and building a cost-conscious culture.
- Raise the bar on sustainability and responsibility including the goal to operate in a carbon neutral value chain by 2040.
- Unlock the full potential of its people.

The fifth priority of the strategy is to become the best-connected brewer. To achieve this, HEINEKEN® will digitally transform its route to the consumer whilst modernising and simplifying the IT landscape. This shift encompasses a range of areas: data driven insights and foresights, digital customer channels including B2B commerce, and simplification and automation of internal processes such as finance and supply chain. One of the fundamental transformations of the IT landscape will be the delivery of a secure digital backbone, which comprises a leaner, single, global Enterprise Resource Planning platform (ERP) connected to a number of modern cloud business platforms providing specialist functional capabilities in supply chain, commerce, and other support functions. Breno recognises that people and culture are at the heart of digital transformation and promotes digital literacy and talent diversity to accelerate change.

Developing the digital core

HEINEKEN®'s global IT landscape has evolved in the past via the implementation of different local ERPs in response to local business needs. Now, in order to achieve harmonisation, speed, and efficiency, the IT group started a digital backbone strategy consisting of a lean single SAP ERP—the new digital core for the business—combined with several modern cloud business platforms. Breno believes any future ERP system should be slimmed down in size and functionality so that it can enable greater organisational agility. This approach supports a fast and flexible response to continuously evolving business conditions.

Monolithic ERP implementations are tricky to transition. The end result of such an approach over time is often spaghetti rather than neatly fitting Lego bricks. Breno is convinced that the simplest and most effective approach to a future ERP landscape is to select niche SaaS business platform offerings that complement the digital core. But he also recognises that a cloud-first strategy has risk in costs and benefits if not carefully managed. He advises caution and advocates a hybrid approach to the cloud.

Aligning the IT organisation with EverGreen

As a consumer-focused organisation, HEINEKEN® follows a market-centric model which translates to empowerment of its operating companies, which are the local markets. IT has a structure that consists of a central group in Amsterdam and Hub in Krakow and lean regional units that operate close to the national operating company businesses. Breno's European team includes about 400 staff, with 90% or more based in the country of the operating company to which they belong. IT managers in these countries report to Breno and the local businesses. He reports to the Group CIO and European business President.

Breno believes and practises the principle of "autonomy with consistency," which in IT means adoption of common platforms providing underlying data and foundational features that are used to develop digital products which can be scaled and reused by many. Examples of these are robotics automation platforms and automation bots.

IT has introduced Agile ways of working globally and continues enhancing its adoption across multiple functions and geographies. Rather than focusing exclusively on processes, Breno believes Agile is a mindset that can be applied to any area of a business.

Defining the qualities of a Master Chef

Breno has three guiding principles that have enabled him to rise to the top of his profession. The first is to be inclusive. He believes everyone on his team has talent, and his role is to provide the space and conditions for them to shine and develop. The second is purposeful communication. IT is at the centre of transformation, so people need to understand the story and their role in simple and meaningful terms. The third is to combine empowerment with action orientation. Being impatient by nature, Breno is keen to see rapid progress towards outcomes.

Having lived and worked in different parts of the world, Breno is acutely aware of cultural differences and the part they play in any transformation journey. Breno is friendly, creative, and adaptable to different cultures. He listens carefully to his staff and makes time for them. Much of his professional satisfaction is derived from constructive dialogue.

Breno believes "our thoughts make up our lives." He uses meditation to monitor his thoughts. This approach provides a valuable sixth sense about work and helps him to avoid problems and reach goals. His advice to next-generation CIOs is to follow their passions and believe in themselves.

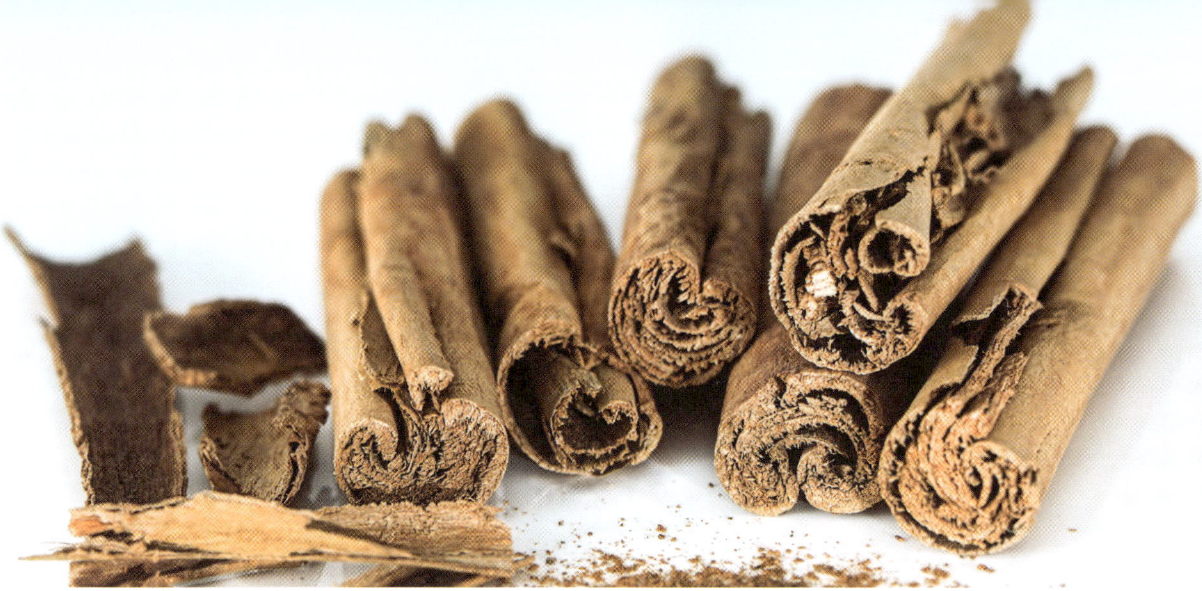

GNV Shipping Line

Undertaking dramatic transformation

Ingredients

- The future can be mapped as a series of short- and long-term initiatives
- The role of CIO should be viewed as a business architect rather than a PC technician
- Walt Disney's guiding motto will be your guide: "If you can dream it, you can do it"

Preparing the dish

Barbara Poli is CIO of Grandi Navi Veloci. Born in a small village in northern Italy, famous for its water, Barbara moved to Milan to take a master's degree in business administration. After university, she worked for consultants KPMG and Accenture, specialising in business strategy. She then spent 11 years in IT and Marketing with Certification and Engineering specialist RINA, rising to the position of CIO and Chief Digital Officer. Three years ago, she left RINA to join GNV and made her home in Genoa.

GNV was created in 1992 by Aldo Grimaldi, initially as a subsidiary of the Grimaldi Group. The first ship of the company, Majestic, entered service in 1993 on the Genoa-Palermo route, followed in 1994 by the sistership, Splendid, on the Genoa-Porto Torres route. Majestic and Splendid were the first ever cruise ferries operated by an Italian company.

The fleet was enlarged with new cruise ferries through the 1990s and the company went public in 2000. In 2010, the company was acquired by the MSC Group and was merged with SNAV, a subsidiary of MSC. Today, the company operates over 20 ferry ships and handles 1.3 million passengers annually.

Learning to turn on a dime

The onset of the coronavirus pandemic created an existential crisis for shipping companies such as GNV. Barbara says the company's top management assembled a special COVID committee to respond to a commercial tsunami. They developed a radical plan of action with both short- and long-term commitments. The first step was triggered by a case of COVID aboard one of the company's cruise liners. This case required immediate action. The company sought alternative accommodation for the passengers. However, in Barbara's words, out of impending tragedy came a ray of opportunity.

GNV converted one of its ferries, Splendid, into a hospital ship to treat coronavirus patients. The ship was delivered to Liguria, Italy, on 23 March 2020, and was made available for the symbolic cost of €1. With help from local and national companies that donated time, materials, and expertise, Splendid was converted into a hospital ship in just 10 days.

The conversion process took place in three distinct stages. The first day was spent undertaking concept design. The second and third days involved mapping out the processes necessary to operate a hospital, including finding partners to undertake the transformation.

The final five days focused on finishing the build process, with special emphasis on establishing data connectivity and visual-monitoring technology throughout the ship.

At the same time, Barbara organised a company-wide move to home working, which had to be completed in similarly tight deadlines. The successful completion of these projects gave Barbara and her IT team a sense of confidence and respect within the organisation, which has helped engender support for long-term transformation initiatives.

Changing the status quo

Punctuality is the hallmark of a successful freight and passenger shipping company, but this can be a tough goal to achieve because of a range of external factors. Such factors include timely access to port-docking stations, onboarding passengers and freight, dealing with customs, and coping with unexpected events, such as healthcare issues and poor weather conditions. Barbara says the best solution to these challenges is to gather information across the external factors that affect the business. This data can then be used to make real-time decisions.

Barbara initiated a company-wide project to create a single control room that resembles NASA's

"If you can dream it, you can do it."

Barbara Poli, CIO, Grandi Navi Veloci

Scan code to watch the full interview.

mission centre. She appointed a team of internal staff and external partners to undertake the design of this new nerve centre. Once again, she adopted a staged approach. The first stage involved workshops and interviews with experts from shipping and other sectors. Her team used this insight to create a minimum viable product of a modern control centre.

A critical aspect during the development of the centre was adopting a data-driven approach. Data had to be collected from legacy systems within GNV, sensors embedded within the company's ships, and external feeds such as weather. However, the IT team rose to the challenge successfully. The data-led approach brought a completely new strategy to operations management that was based on real-time decision making. Barbara estimates the financial benefits of the control centre were as high as €4M through year one.

Defining the role of a Master Chef

Having come from a business background, Barbara was delighted to enter IT and help bring technology and the rest of the organisation together. She brought a "can-do" attitude, which has been reflected in the success of her recent projects, such as creation of the hospital and control tower. Barbara's mantra is: "If you can dream it, you can do it." She often makes heavy demands on herself and the people around her. She is also keen to challenge conventional wisdom by harnessing new technologies, such as the Internet of Things and data analytics, to solve difficult business problems.

When Barbara became CIO at GNV, the IT team was initially confused by her change-driven personal style. She recognised quickly that there were two types of people: those who embrace change, and those who cannot accept it. This recognition enabled her to select appropriate talent for the company's change projects. She used the rest of the department to deliver reliable IT services.

Barbara's main source of satisfaction is to do more each day. She learnt from her mother to value independence, follow her dreams, and become a warrior. She refers to a quote from Nelson Mandela: "I never lose. I either win or learn." Her advice to next-generation leaders is to learn how to harness the power of new technologies to service the business.

FIVE
STRATEGY & INNOVATION

Productivity and revenue growth have been at a virtual standstill across Europe for the past two decades due in part to an obsession with the delivery of internal efficiencies. In this subsection, the two Master Chefs from Prosegur, a Spanish security company, and Red Hat, a pioneering technology specialist, adopt a philosophy of constantly looking outwards as well as inwards.

That's a radical change because executives in mature sectors such as security and information technology have focused historically on modernising existing business processes in preference to creating the new. This concentration has often resulted in a zero-sum gain. However, our Cookbook shows that the adoption of automation and cloud platforms can help companies improve internal efficiencies while also embracing innovation.

Prosegur recognised its security services were highly manual and in urgent need of modernisation. The company applied automation techniques such as RPA, optical character recognition, and natural language recognition to boost operational efficiency. Prosegur also applied a philosophy of open innovation to harness new business ideas from its own staff and external partners, which generated a growing pipeline of new opportunities for revenue growth.

Red Hat has fostered the concept of open innovation since its inception in 1993. Its open-source platforms are a work of constant iteration and the company sources ideas from thousands of developers across the open-source community. These ideas generate new sources of differentiation and innovation. Red Hat's Master Chef emphasises the need to apply standard solutions based on open-source technologies to simplify structures and enable rapid scaling.

Prosegur

Remodelling the business at scale

Ingredients

- The "modernising the factory" business model must be separated from "creating the new"
- Modernisation requires standard technology platforms and data harmonisation
- "Creating the new" requires a separate team that experiments with emerging technologies

Preparing the dish

Javier Cabrerizo is Group Managing Director of global security company Prosegur. He has an MBA from INSEAD Business School and completed several programs on Innovation and Transformation Strategy from Harvard and MIT. His career developed in three stages: helping to launch tech start-ups in Europe and USA, such as Meta4 and NewKnow, working 10 years with Oracle in California and Europe, and leading Prosegur's transformation to becoming a more tech intensive company.

Prosegur was founded in 1976 as a private security company, with a focus on power plants, industrial facilities, and shopping centres. In 1987, it became the first security company to list on the Madrid Stock Exchange and remains the largest private security company in Spain and third in the world. Prosegur operates in 26 countries with 150,000 staff.

In 2017, Prosegur demerged its cash business, which listed separately on the Madrid Stock Exchange.

Prosegur Cash remains majority owned by Prosegur. The company's expansion has often been via acquisition. Its operations grew initially through Spain, Portugal, and Latin America, but the company has since expanded to other parts of Europe and Asia. Prosegur holds a market-leading position in many of the countries in which it operates, including Spain, Brazil and Germany.

Transforming the current operating model

Javier recognised he had two related tasks ahead of him when he joined Prosegur. First, transforming the operating model of the existing business via the introduction of automation and standardisation. Second, increasing revenues by introducing an innovation model to develop and scale new products and services. Technology would play a central role in both tasks.

Javier recognised that Prosegur's rapid growth, which was due to more than 100 acquisitions, created a diversity of systems and data structures. He harmonised the technology foundation by adopting a new architecture and a move to public cloud platforms. This shift enabled him to reduce the company's legacy debt and introduce standards across countries and regions. However, he also recognised that flexibility at the country level was key to exploiting market conditions successfully.

Having standardised the technology platform, Javier focused on four mission-critical processes to streamline the business: hire-to-retire, customer journey, supply chain, and finance. He searched for and deployed best practices from external sources, such as using Microsoft Dynamics for CRM and Oracle Cloud for ERP. He also ensured each primary business received technological solutions that were appropriate to their markets while also harmonising data at the corporate level.

Javier employed robotic process automation to eliminate repetitive manual tasks that slow the business down. He is now extending the capabilities of RPA by introducing optical character recognition, natural language recognition, and machine learning. These initiatives will help reduce costs while boosting customer and employee experiences across the globe.

Introducing an innovation model

Javier says successful businesses look outwards as well as inwards. They constantly reinvent products and services to match changes in the marketplace. Javier adopts an "open" approach that helps Prosegur engage with external sources of innovation, such as start-ups and universities. He has created

"The best ideas derive from employees who know what is going on."

Javier Cabrerizo Barrera, Group Managing Director, Prosegur

Scan code to watch the full interview.

a central team to manage this task, with strong links to individual countries and business units. He has also established a venture fund of €30 million to kickstart new opportunities.

One way of feeding the innovation model has been to invite ideas from within the organisation. Through an innovation challenge programme, 7,000 staff have generated more than 1,000 new ideas. One internal innovation involved using visual analytics to differentiate between real and false alarms, such as a dog moving within a house, while one external innovation involved working with a start-up to create COVID-free office environments by monitoring people density and social distancing.

Javier says, "the best ideas derive from employees who know what is going on." Similar to the Toyota Production System philosophy that has revolutionised the automotive sector, employees can make incremental improvements that create big productivity gains over time. When significant new ideas emerge, Javier is happy to deploy funding and give staff space to pursue them.

In all cases, Javier expects innovations to be built using standard platforms and harmonised data sources to exploit Prosegur's economies of scale.

Being an effective leader

Javier has three main roles at Prosegur: overseeing product innovation, modernising the IT platform, and managing administrative processes, such as finance and HR. IT is integral to driving operational efficiency and creating new products. Software is now central to product innovation and revenue growth, making it a key component of a successful business strategy.

Javier recognises the need to pick top performers for his management team. He looks for talent that is proven to be best in class at what they do. He sets the vision, context, and direction for his team, but expects them to "fly on their own." He places people in demanding positions and acknowledges that the role of a modern business leader is to show up in a crisis and make difficult decisions.

Defining the role of a Master Chef

Trust plays a big part in Javier's leadership style. He expects his team to have full confidence in the direction he sets. Javier says, "Leadership is something that people give to you," rather than coming from hierarchical authority structures. Leaders must connect with the rhythm of the business and understand how fast it can move. Pushing the pedal too hard creates resistance. Leaders must be sensitive to the impact of change.

Javier's personal mantra is based on the approach of Roman emperor Marcus Aurelius and includes a focus on objectivity, selfless action, and an ability to accept reality. He tells the next generation of leaders to be the best people they can be. As situations in business become more complex, success is about delving deeply into problems and having the patience to resolve these challenges.

Red Hat

Turning innovation into a compelling transformation story

Ingredients

- Leaders must work out where to standardise and where to innovate
- Leaders should be clear, kind, and make space for other folks
- Leaders tell people stories about the work they do and its impact, so they can be heroes

Preparing the dish

Gunnar Hellekson is Vice President and General Manager for Linux. He studied theatre and computer science at Drew University in New Jersey. After working for several start-ups, Gunnar joined Red Hat in 2006, working in sales for the government sector, eventually becoming CTO for the public sector group. After a stint running product management for Red Hat Enterprise Linux, he moved into his current role in November 2021.

Red Hat is an American enterprise software company with an open-source development model. The company's mission statement is to be a catalyst in communities of customers, partners, and developers who are creating better software the open-source way. Since its inception in 1993, Red Hat has placed open-source innovation at the core of its culture.

Balancing standardisation and innovation

Gunnar is responsible for the product management of Enterprise Linux. His work leads him to believe modern

"Be clear, kind, and make space for other folks."

Gunnar Hellekson, Vice President and General Manager for Linux

Scan code to watch the full interview.

digital leaders face a range of business challenges. He refers to the OODA Loop, a term coined by US military strategist Colonel John Boyd, who suggested people who are trying to execute on a mission must Orient, Observe, Decide, and then Act.

In his theorisation, Boyd suggests the quicker you go through the stages of the OODA Loop, the more effective you will be as a leader. Gunnar says it's important that digital leaders who work through these OODA Loops decide where to standardize and where to innovate. Every IT organisation must decide which elements can be standardised on commoditised platforms and which areas will provide differentiating value through innovation.

Connecting ERP to digital transformation

Although there's tension between standardisation and innovation, Gunnar suggests the good news for digital leaders is that they're also complementary: It's not possible to innovate unless you have a stable platform for change. In many companies, ERP remains the central nervous system of a company, or "the rich Earth" upon which businesses innovate.

Traditional ERP systems are increasingly moving to the public cloud. As this transition happens, it makes sense to use open tools to create richer connections and ecosystems. Gunnar says the skills, practices, and operational disciplines required to move ERP to the cloud are crucial digital transformation capabilities for all companies. Organisations that perfect this shift can place ERP at the heart of a modern, digital business.

Building a robust product

Gunnar says Linux, as the core of the open-source project, remains a constant work in progress. Red Hat has honed the innovation and tools that have emerged from the open-source community to create the operating system Fedora. Thousands of people in the community work alongside Red Hat to continually improve Fedora. The best innovations are sent through to CentOS Stream, which is the next stable version of Red Hat Enterprise Linux.

This iterative process produces a robust operating system. Gunnar's team works to provide direction, making best use of internal engineering resources and ensuring customers and partners are happy with the final product. His work involves a balance between top-down internal planning and keeping a watchful eye on the development work in open-source communities: "It makes for a dynamic but very rewarding work experience."

Leading people

Gunnar says the most important part of his role is providing strong direction and clarity of purpose. He says Red Hat is a meritocratic and flat organisation, so it is crucial people know the end goal and can work autonomously to deliver great results: "I spend a lot of time helping people understand how their work can serve the overall company strategy."

Gunnar visualises his management requirements as a dashboard, with a series of dials and knobs that can be used to watch and then influence different departments, such as product management, marketing, operations, and partners. Access to Red Hat's strong internal engineering team means he can maintain a lean, core team that focuses on telling stories, setting clear goals, and having a great impact on behalf of the business.

Hiring talent

Gunnar says Red Hat "goes out of its way" to hire world-class people who are leaders in open-source projects. He says the company is blessed by being a great place to work, but also by having a mission that talented people are very passionate about: "It's not hard to get people interested in working for Red Hat, especially if they are already working in Linux."

The Red Hat recruitment process allows the company to create an effective balance between the innovation that is happening in broader open-source communities and being able to advocate on behalf of partners and customers. Once hired, new recruits find a fascinating corporate culture—one that rewards self-starters. It might seem chaotic from the outside, but it produces an elaborate system for consensual decision-making.

Defining the qualities of a Master Chef

Above all, Gunnar says he hopes people think of him as a kind leader. People spend most of their waking hours at work and the activities they undertake need to be enjoyable. One of his mantras is: "Be clear, kind, and make space for other folks."

Gunnar relies on frameworks and rubrics. People must understand their work and the impact it has. If you don't give people a story about the work they do, they'll create their own stories: "I tell them a story about the work they do—and it's a story where they can be a hero."

He uses meditation and thinks of himself as a systems thinker with strong principles. He enjoys taking problems, turning them around, and looking at them from different angles. As part of that process, he's reluctant to make hasty decisions. Given the significant heritage of Red Hat, he says it's crucial his team members are thoughtful and deliberate about everything they do.

Vegetarian Korean Bibimbap

Serves 2

- 200g firm pressed tofu
- 4 tsp light soya sauce or tamari
- 1 tsp Gochujang (Korean chilli paste)
- 4 tsp sesame or rice bran oil
- 100g of shitake mushrooms
- 100g fresh spinach
- 80g soya bean sprouts
- 1 carrot shredded
- 50g edamame bean
- ½ cup brown or white rice, cooked
- ½ long cucumber, finely sliced
- 1 spring onion, finely sliced
- 1 egg (optional)

Pickled Daikon

- 100g daikon (or radishes)
- 60 ml rice wine vinegar
- 60–120 ml water
- 2 Tbsp sugar, adjust to taste
- 1 tsp kosher salt, adjust to taste

Bibimbap means "mixed rice" and is an iconic Korean meal-in-a-bowl. This dish can be traced back to the late 19th century. It's been suggested the dish was a tradition for farmers during the harvest season, as it can be easily made in large quantities to feed families and farmhands.

The unique feature of bibimbap is the visual and active participation of mixing the beautifully laid out sauteed vegetables (called namul) atop a steaming bowl of rice and mixing it with the umami dressing that gives this dish its spicy kick. An egg is usually cracked on top prior to serving which adds to the gooey, eggy goodness, and the act of finishing the dish's preparation yourself offers a ritual that heightens the anticipation of enjoying your first mouthful.

Bibimbap can be enjoyed throughout the year as a vegetarian meal, or sliced beef or pork can also be added for the meat lovers. The centre piece consists of seasonal sauteed vegetables which can vary from beans and bracken fern stems (gosari) to roots, flowers, petals, or fruits. They can be prepared blanched, fried, steamed, boiled, or eaten raw. The magic that brings this dish together is the Gochujang sauce (Korean's answer to chilli) that adds a distinctive flavour.

To start, cut a pressed block of tofu into equal size cubes, then pour soy sauce it (mixed in with 1 tsp of Gochujang). Set the tofu aside for at least 30 minutes to allow it to absorb the marinade. Heat up 2 tsp of sesame or bran oil on a non-stick pan and place the marinated tofu cubes into the hot oil. Fry, turning frequently until browned on all sides. Prepare the mushroom by frying them gently, and once brown, add the spinach with a splash of water and cook it on low heat until all excess water cooks out. Boil the soya bean sprout and then season all the sauteed vegetables with toasted sesame oil, salt, and white pepper to taste.

The best accompaniment to Bibimbap is the pickled daikon. Slice the daikon into thin slices and place them in a jar. Bring rice vinegar, water (60–120 ml depending how acidic you like your pickles), sugar, and salt to a gentle boil.

The favourite dish of Gunnar Hellekson

Dressing

- 2 Tbsp Gochujang (Korean chilli paste)
- 2 tsp rice wine vinegar
- 1 Tbsp soy sauce or tamari
- 1 Tbsp toasted sesame oil
- 1 Tbsp maple syrup or cane sugar
- 1 small garlic clove, finely grated

Pour the hot pickling liquid over the daikon. The pickles can be eaten straight away, but they are worth making a day in advance as their flavour develops with time. Store in an airtight jar in the fridge.

Make the dressing by whisking all dressing ingredients together in a medium size bowl. To serve, divide all the veggies and cooked tofu between two bowls. Sprinkle with sesame seeds and top with the Gochujang dressing and "Mashikeh-Mogoseyo" (which means "enjoy your meal" in Korean).

PLAYBOOK 3

THE DATA PLAYBOOK FOR WINE CONNOISSEURS

The crucial role of data assets and analytics in an uncertain economy

Data volumes are exploding in our modern, hyper-connected and increasingly hyper-personalised world. But our ability to harness value from data remains elusive, with market estimates suggesting 80% of big data projects fail to deliver tangible business outcomes.

Failure to deliver value from data projects is not an option. Traditional organisations are under increasing pressure to compete with digital natives in every sector. While the challenge from these fast-moving upstarts is huge, blue-chip enterprises hold a trump card. By harnessing data assets accumulated over decades, incumbents should have an unassailable advantage against digital newcomers. So, how can C-suite executives at major companies realise full value from their currently fragmented data assets?

What's clear is that the right architecture and framework can help CIOs and their C-suite colleagues to harvest game-changing insight from data. Business leaders who develop a mature approach to data become wine connoisseurs. Across the full insight-generation journey—from fermentation to blending and onto tasting—the generation of valuable data is like the creation of a fine wine.

CIOs and their business peers must embrace the opportunities that information holds and become true mixologists for the emerging data-driven economy. Now is the time to develop a taste for data-led change.

A changing business context

As we accelerate through a period of dramatic technological change, we are witnessing a global transition from "analogue" to "digital" organisations.

Our contention is that this transition is changing every business process.

You might feel your organisation has not transitioned to the digital era. If so, you're not alone. Few members of the Global 1000 conform to this new digital norm. Yet, at the same time, digital-native behemoths, such as the FAANG (Facebook, Apple, Amazon, Netflix, and Google) group, have adopted structures and services that allow them to hyper-scale and innovate continuously due to their data-centric business models.

Traditional organisations must evolve rapidly from analogue to digital to survive and flourish. Mastering data assets is at the heart of their future success.

Key business metrics that matter

When traditional organisations become data-driven, they can deliver exceptional growth, profitability, and quality at the pace of digital natives. This tight grip on data enables them to enjoy better equity returns as well as higher customer and employee satisfaction.

Before the introduction of digital technology in the 1990s, companies needed to excel in just one of three disciplines—product innovation, operational excellence, or customer intimacy—to achieve commercial success, as defined in Treacy and Wiersema's seminal work, Market Disciplines of Market Leaders.

Today, success is multifaceted. According to Dr. Joe Weinman in his recent book Digital Disciplines, digital natives can achieve excellence in all three disciplines by creating data-centric structures and processes.

While digital natives have achieved new levels of success, incumbents have moved at a much slower pace. Reengineering, lean thinking, process mining, and digital transformation have contributed to incremental performance improvements within analogue organisations. However, C-suite executives are rightly demanding more radical change. As Michael Hammer said in the 1990s: "It is not about the 5% but about the 500% improvement."

Progressive organisations are making this step change. They are applying digital techniques to grow their operations rapidly while also improving outcomes for their customers.

The decision-making process is the place to start

CEOs and CFOs now acknowledge that "data-driven" decision-making processes lie at the heart of high-performance organisations.

Data-driven organisations publish all their information so it's accessible to all parties on close to a real-time basis. Successful businesses create a fabric that enables staff to access multiple sources of information for decision-making processes instead of restricting them to limited data sets.

Whether you are innovating products, streamlining operations, or improving customer experiences, decision-making processes need to be close to real-time, reliable, and predictive. Senior managers can't rely on historical trends or intuitions. Digital businesses depend entirely on their data to achieve excellence across all disciplines.

How to redesign decision-making processes

As IT professionals, we have been preoccupied for decades with process reengineering and its many tools, such as lean thinking, process mining, and value mapping. It's time for this obsession to end.

The reality today is that many process-reengineering efforts fail because they become technology-led projects. Too often, these projects focus on micro-process components rather than end-to-end workflows that deliver measurable value.

Data-driven decision making is

a process. It incorporates a data pipeline that starts with collection and integration and ends with deployment and analytics. We believe the delivery of a successful redesign requires a proven framework, known as "DataOps." This framework has three key factors:

1. Technologies and related tooling that support a data-driven business model and make data available to all employees
2. A culture where everyone buys into the idea of using data to make decisions at every level of the organisation (from the front line up to the main board)
3. An organisation that supports empowerment and collaboration across the organisation, especially those working on the front line

What changes are required in IT to support a data-driven approach?

DataOps is similar to its namesake DevOps—it favours multidisciplinary teams, an Agile philosophy, and rapid sprints. However, DataOps is broader in its nature. First, it brings non-technical and technical people together to define a business goal. From here, DataOps helps to define objectives and capabilities. Finally, DataOps helps extract insights from data. This combination of benefits delivers desired business outcomes.

DataOps is also an umbrella term that refers to the collection of technical practices, workflows, cultural norms, and architectural patterns that will allow an organisation to integrate its data assets into its business goals and processes. While each organisation's data pipelines are configured differently, DataOps enables four core capabilities within a company:

1. Rapid innovation, experimentation, and testing to deliver data insights to users and customers
2. Improved data quality with extremely low error rates
3. Synchronized collaboration across teams of people, environments, and technologies
4. Orchestrated monitoring of data pipelines to ensure clear measurements and transparent results

Embracing DataOps requires a fundamental shift in approach. To enable such a successful data-driven environment, an IT organisation will need to change its operating model from waterfall and on-premises to DevOps and multi-cloud platforms.

Within this broader macro-framework, there are several other trends associated with data itself that need to be embraced in a shift to DataOps:

- Scale-up data storage combines with scale-out data storage, enabled by graphics processing units (GPUs)
- Data structures move from centralised to distributed, aided by software-defined storage to edge, core, and cloud
- Data analytics adopts artificial intelligence and machine learning to achieve predictive outcomes
- Data input spans verbal, visual, and virtual information, aided by natural language processing and machine vision

Setting yourself up for success as a data mixologist

The explanation for the failure rate of data projects is simple: many of these initiatives are too ambitious and lack proper orchestration between IT and lines of business. We suggest that data projects should proceed at a more incremental pace, with tighter business governance. This approach accelerates time to value and reduces the risk of failure.

Any organisation that wants to become data-enabled or data-driven must ensure the correct governance and skills are in place. Standards and frameworks also need to be defined. In addition, effective communications between IT and lines of business must be established.

Moving from a traditional on-premises and waterfall IT environment to a DataOps operating model requires a wholesale transformation of business and IT resources and capabilities. For example, traditional ERP skills relating to SAP and Oracle need to be complemented by expertise in Agile software development and data science.

Sourcing this specialist capability in today's competitive digital labour market can be extremely challenging. That's where CIONET Cookbooks can help—they describe the attributes of successful digital leaders and their teams in a data-driven business environment.

Six recommendations to operate data-driven business models

IT has a critical but not exclusive role in helping traditional organisations transition to a data-driven business model. Modern digital leaders must recognise their key position in achieving this vital transition.

Here are six best-practice recommendations that emerge from practical experiences drawn from the CIONET European community of 10,000 digital leaders:

1. Envision how businesses can move to "everything as a service" by enhancing products and customer channels using software and data.
2. Help solve wider business problems by identifying how modern tools, such as DataOps and DevOps, can generate innovative solutions.
3. Promote a set of winning stories that can stimulate conversations with business partners and engender trust and confidence.
4. Adopt suitable IT processes and architectures that enable business staff to access the right data in the right place at the right time.
5. Attract and motivate data science specialists to tackle business problems and identify opportunities with tangible outcomes in mind.
6. Engage with an ecosystem of partners that includes both technical and vertical business skills.

PLAYBOOK 4

TOWARDS THE FULLY AUTOMATED ENTERPRISE

Intelligent automation technologies are maturing, and CIOs should make efforts to assess and deploy these tools as quickly as possible

What once seemed possible is now probable: by embracing intelligent automation, enterprises can create a technology-led step change in performance and productivity. To make that shift, CIOs must demonstrate the value of automation and help the rest of the business turn intelligent automation into a competitive advantage.

As part of our ongoing research programme, CIONET has examined how digital leaders are applying intelligent automation to evaluate where technologies such as robotic process automation, artificial intelligence, and low code/no code can accelerate the reinvention of business and the redesign of work.

While our research suggests intelligent automation is still at an early stage, the CIOs we have spoken with also indicate it already heralds a fundamental change in the way businesses operate. IT organisations will provide the platforms, education, and orchestration for automation, process mining, and associated technologies, while the various functions across the business will adopt a "citizen's development" charter based on low code/no code.

However, this pattern we describe above is far from set in stone. Intelligent automation will continue to evolve rapidly. CIOs have an urgent duty to inform their peers of the huge potential of this technology and to provide the necessary governance and test environments to evaluate and guide its development during the next five to ten years.

What are the different approaches to intelligent automation?

Over the past few decades, fruitless paths have been trodden on the journey towards the fully automated enterprise. Think, for example of the following techniques: reengineering in the nineties, workflow automation in the noughties, and lean thinking and total quality management. And yet, despite the application of all these techniques, productivity in Europe has flatlined during the past 20 years.

These failings are becoming ever-more pressing. As we enter the new era of "winner takes all" that has been pioneered by fleet-of-foot digital natives, CIOs at incumbent organisations need an innovative approach to boost productivity and sponsor growth. So, how will they escape from the productivity and innovation traps that have haunted business leaders for decades?

Avoiding these pitfalls will not be straightforward. Our research suggests there are many barriers to overcome, such as legacy systems and processes, fragmentation of vital data assets, ponderous decision cycles, and a lack of skills. However, it is crucial to recognise our CIO community is adamant that none of these obstacles are insurmountable.

CIONET members are already pursuing a range of initiatives to help modernise systems and streamline processes. These include short-term, tactical fixes and longer-term redesigns:

1. Pathways to automation: Applying short-term fixes

A more fundamental redesign of business processes can take years to complete. However, companies must find short-term fixes to reduce costs and speed up critical processes to both satisfy ever-more demanding customers and stave off competition from digital natives. Here are some tactical approaches that CIOs are taking:

- Using RPA to eliminate repetitive, manual tasks in current processes, such as data entry and data manipulation
- Overlaying a data integration layer across fragmented systems to create transparency across supply chains
- Bridging legacy systems, such as monolithic ERP systems, to modern applications

2. Pathways to automation: Using strategic approaches to process redesign

CIONET members recognise that their core systems and critical business processes are not designed to compete with digital natives. Fundamental change is required, but this will take years to complete. Incumbents, therefore, need to take a staged approach to automation.

CIOs suggest the main pathways to modernisation include selecting two to three critical processes from the many hundreds that exist in large organisations and undertaking a complete redesign.

3. Pathways to automation: Adopting more holistic approaches

An attempt to modernise the processes associated with today's factory might not be sufficient to help incumbents compete with digital natives. In these cases, incumbents might need to take radical action, replacing their legacy systems entirely or adopting entirely new models. Examples include:

- Migrating applications to the public cloud and adopting

- Software as a Service, which opens possibilities for new organisational designs and associated services
- Building entirely new processing factories based on digital business models and microservices, without disrupting current business flows

How are RPA and associated tools being applied today?

According to the CIONET community, RPA and associated technologies—such as AI, machine learning, and process mining—are still at the early stage of maturity. Our research suggests 20 to 100 robots are typically installed within large organisations.

Those kinds of numbers don't look huge in the context of a business that employs thousands of people. However, these initial deployments highlight how pioneering business leaders are already exploring automation that can boost performance and productivity:

1. Creating further internal efficiencies by automating repetitive tasks and focusing staff on value-based activities
2. Offering new and effective ways to interact with customers by applying chatbots and natural language processing in call centres
3. Accelerating modernisation by providing an interim bridge between heritage and modern applications, while organisations replace legacy systems

What is the CIO's role in intelligent automation?

The case for automation is clear—large organisations need to reduce costs and improve speed to market to compete with more agile and streamlined digital natives. As automation technologies mature, RPA and an associated range of AI tools will provide the means for action. There is no room for complacency. CIOs must prepare for a fully automated enterprise.

1. Review and upgrade critical business process design

Although many past attempts have been made to use technology to improve the processes that businesses undertake, CIOs see modern process-mining tools as a step change when it comes to uncovering bottlenecks. Here are some key processes that are being redesigned:

- For manufacturing companies, process redesign is focused on product innovation and in-service maintenance
- For banks, process redesign focuses on customer on-boarding and loan authorisations
- For insurance companies, process redesign focuses on claims processing and policy management

2. Introduce standardisation across organisations

Organisations with complex structures that reach across multiple business lines and territories see process redesign as an ideal opportunity to increase standardisation of business processes and operating procedures. Several CIOs have set up group boards to oversee such activities and are looking for further scale efficiencies:

- Adopting common process designs between national affiliates
- Harmonising processes within functions, such as finance and HR
- Adopting open platform standards to accelerate post-merger integration

3. Pilot and scale RPA applications

Organisations are deploying RPA and AI in a range of areas right now to assess the potential benefits and build cases for full-scale rollouts. As part of this process, they often create a Centre of Excellence (CoE) to pilot and scale RPA. The role of the CoE includes:

- Developing and applying a structured approach to

process mapping that can quantify benefits, including cost reduction and improved responsiveness

- Providing people and training to business units, so they become more self-sufficient
- Financing local projects to encourage the business units on the automation journey
- Forming global agreements with vendors and their automation technologies to obtain pricing discounts and consistency of usage across the group
- Building a library of assets such as APIs that can be accessed by local businesses

4. Implement effective guardrails

RPA and AI will bring in a new era of citizen development. Although this era should help to accelerate the development of new applications, it also brings risks that IT will need to mitigate. Technology teams will play a key role in helping to educate the rest of the business about automation:

- The cost of purchasing and maintaining thousands of semi-autonomous robots, each engaged in different tasks across the organisation
- The possibility of pockets of grey IT, as users develop their own applications and data sets away from the gaze of the technology department
- The necessary response by IT to establish suitable guardrails to enable interworking and to adopt a cross-organisation automation platform for RPA

What are the next steps towards the fully automated enterprise?

CIOs across Europe suggest RPA and associated technologies offer a new pathway towards the fully automated enterprise. While these technologies are at an early stage of maturity, some companies are already generating value from RPA. These successful implementations highlight how intelligent automation can make a dramatic difference to how enterprises operate, but only if IT organisations become involved as early as possible.

Automation will need careful governance to ensure beneficial outcomes. CIOs should be custodians of intelligent automation. They should make active efforts to assess and deploy automation tools, and provide governance, education, and platform support to their business partners. In such a situation, CIOs should undertake the following actions:

1. Evaluate RPA, AI, and process mining through controlled pilots, sponsored where possible at group level. Examine appropriate platforms that will enable the scaling up of RPA as and when value is proven.
2. Inform peers in the C-suite of the potential opportunities and benefits that automation brings. Agree on an appropriate roadmap.
3. Work with lines of business to explore and test low code/ no code approaches towards intelligent automation.

PLAYBOOK 5

CLOSING THE INNOVATION GAP

Incumbent organisations need a new approach to innovation that is scalable, creative, and which brings senior executives together

C-suite executives are under huge pressure to deliver change. Digital leaders such as CIOs, CTOs and CDOs are making every effort to mobilise innovation initiatives within their organisations. Equally, the CEO community is under pressure to demonstrate how it can generate billions of dollars of new value through genuine innovation activities. The heat is most definitely on.

Yet despite these valiant efforts, the accelerating pace of technology developments and the exploding number of digital natives emerging in virtually every sector, large incumbents remain slow to respond to existential threats. The FTSE 100 Index in the UK today is at similar levels to 1999.

We believe there is a way to overcome this roadblock. Our research reveals an ever-widening gap between what CEOs and their technology executives mean by innovation and how best to implement successful change programmes. There are numerous examples of innovation activities among incumbent organisations, be they incubators, accelerators, joint ventures, or start-ups. But none have shifted the revenue or profit dials significantly during the past two decades. A case in point: just 5% of S&P 500 companies surpassed annual growth rates of 5% between 2009 and 2014.

At CIONET, we believe business leaders require a common language for innovation. This common language will help technology leaders to be productive innovation partners to the CEO and other members of the C-suite. But making this step change requires a clear CEO vision, C-level empowerment, and an appropriate set of resources. So, how can we make that happen?

Our research suggests four critical success factors will help C-suite leaders to find a common language and close an ever-widening innovation gap. We present these below before, followed by a showcase interview with Javier Cabrerizo, who is Group Managing Director of global security company Prosegur. At a time when the demand for innovation has never been greater, Javier has placed technology-led change at the heart of his company's business. What's more, the approach is paying big dividends.

We believe all digital leaders and their C-suite peers can learn from Javier's innovation language. Before we turn to our showcase profile of his pioneering work, let's consider the four critical success factors that will help traditional business to close the innovation gap and deliver digital programmes that deliver great results.

Four critical success factors to help close the innovation gap

Organisations wedded to traditional structures based on operational excellence might continue to deliver profit for years to come, but they will be faced with gradual extinction as new digital players enter their territories. We believe there are four factors that can improve the odds in favour of success with respect to innovation programmes:

1. CEO commitment to innovation

The CEO must be committed to fundamental change and innovation must become the top enterprise priority. Most CEOs we speak with are frustrated with current innovation programmes that appear to tinker with the status quo rather than deliver genuine transformation. We believe that, as with any major change programme, CEOs need to take big risks, accept failures when they occur, and lead in the application of new technologies. Timing is critical as well as resilience to setbacks.

CEOs should set stretched business targets and communicate repeatedly to drive an innovation culture. The board must establish a senior-level steering committee that can oversee direction. All functions, especially HR, Finance, and IT, should support the innovation programme. Broader stakeholder involvement needs to be achieved through extensive communications programmes. Any senior executives who stands in the way of progress should be moved sideways or dismissed.

2. Scalable learning rather than scalable efficiency

With a pedigree in practicing operational excellence over decades, large incumbents continue to pursue relentless standardisation to reduce the possibility of failure. Real exponential learning cannot occur without accepting failures as well as successes. Scalable learning is essential if organisations want to operate at the edge against digital natives.

3. Changes to the organisational model

The task for most organisations is to transition from analogue structures based on stable processes and systems to digital structures that are designed for agility and speed. The latter are often characterised by small customer-facing teams, micro-service components, and digital platforms, such as at Amazon and Google. This transition might be possible at the core of today's enterprises but is more likely at the edge through the adoption of new business models and associated technologies.

A dedicated executive at senior level should lead innovation activities on behalf of the entire organisation. They should be supported by a small team that has access to a substantial budget to fund developments. Performance should be tracked and reported to the CEO on at least a monthly basis. The innovation team should involve customers as well as trade partners in all its activities. Legacy issues should be addressed at the outset with enough funding to remove such obstacles.

4. A new role for the CIO

IT is frequently tasked with running the back office of the organisation, delivering projects on time, and then innovating if there is any spare budget left. CIOs who are serious about innovation must embed technology-enabled change into all their company's products and services. They will need to ring-fence traditional operational activities so that they can concentrate on business innovation. This positioning will require strong external partnerships.

CIOs should review the current IT organisation to ensure it can deliver Agile solutions at scale to its business partners and enterprise customers. New skills and infrastructural facilities might need to be generated internally or bought in. Successful migration to the cloud will be important in delivering digital IT capability.

Equally, CIOs should evaluate and test emerging technologies to keep the business ahead of the technology curve.

Our view is that successful CIOs might opt to join a new ventures team at group level to focus on breakthrough innovations. This approach will help avoid organisational inertia back in the core.

A case for action

Javier Cabrerizo has made innovation central to his successful leadership approach. However, not every digital leader is as far-sighted. CIONET research highlights the growing gap between expectations and realities for business innovation at large incumbents. Too many organisations still play around with small-scale innovation activities that cannot move the growth needle significantly.

Failures in the retail sector are a good example. Too many high-street retailers were slow to recognise the power of e-commerce, as demonstrated most clearly by Amazon's one-click approach. The same slow pace of change has been repeated at incumbents in other sectors. Take the IT industry, where an inability to recognise the power of the cloud has marginalised many traditional players.

Only the chief executive can close the innovation gap. Change is all about vision, leadership, and the ability to gain consensus. However, the IT community has an important role to play in bringing new developments and possibilities to the attention of the CEO. Digital leaders must lay the foundation on which successful innovation can take place.

It is our profound hope that this message resonates among the 7,000 digital leaders within the CIONET community and creates the necessary collective case for action. As our IT Cookbook for 2022 demonstrates, there are Master Chefs such as Javier who are able to give their CEOs a taste for the game-changing power of innovation. Everyone can learn from these talented professionals.

Dutch Sea bass with vegetables and Gouda mash

Serves 2 portions

- Whole sea bass (400 to 600g per piece, deveined and descaled)
- 2 tomatoes
- 3 fennels
- 1 thick carrot
- 1 shallot
- 2 garlic cloves
- 6 artichoke hearts
- 150g small, pitted olives
- 100g rosemary
- Few sprigs of fresh oregano
- Few sprigs of chives (or parsley)
- Olive oil
- Ground cracked pepper
- 10g capers
- 2 tsp coarse salt

The favourite dish of Guido Lemeire

You can see many variations of this classic fish dish in cuisines around the world. Mediterranean people love to accompany their fish dishes with generous lashing of fresh tomatoes and herbs. The Chinese like to steam their fish covered in fresh sliced ginger, soya sauce, and Shaoxing Chinese wine. The Indians cook their fish with spices and curry leaves in tamarind or coconut-based curries. In this Dutch inspired fish recipe, we are going for the classical approach with the whole sea bass as the centre piece. You can also use other white fish like trout, cod, or snapper, but adjust the cooking time for each of the different types of fishes.

Preheat the oven to 200°C. Check that the fish has been deveined and descaled carefully. Scrape from the tail towards the head with a sharp chef's knife. Then rinse the scraped scales off the fish.

Rub some salt over the fish and rinse it after to prepare the fish.

Peel the shallots and cut them into coarse strips or shreds. Roughly chop the tomatoes. Cut the fennel into thin strips or in a julienne style and remove the tough heart at the stem of the vegetable. Do the same with the peeled carrot. This will add colour, texture, and flavour to the dish.

Put a roasting pan on your stove. Heat over a medium heat and pour in a generous amount of good olive oil. The olive oil will become the "sauce" for the fish to sit in, so it's essential to use the best olive oil you can find. Place the shallot, fennel, carrots, and tomato pieces in the roasting tin along with the crushed garlic cloves. Let the vegetables simmer, stirring occasionally. Add some freshly ground pepper and a little salt. Cut the artichoke hearts into large bite-sized pieces and spread them together with the vegetables, then add the capers and the small, pitted olives. Break and rub your rosemary sprigs and oregano together between your palm to release the oil, then add the rest of the herbs over the tray, mixing everything together thoroughly. Season to taste with pepper and a pinch of coarse salt.

Cut the tail and fins off the sea bass and place the fish on top of the stewed vegetables. Season them with some freshly ground salt and pepper. Place the roasting pan in the hot oven at 200°C and cook the fish with vegetables

Gouda Mash

- 800g potatoes boiled
- 2 Egg yolks
- 6 tsp butter
- 150g Whole milk
- 120g gouda cheese grated
- Fresh chopped parsley for garnish

for about 15 minutes. If you have an oven grill, it would be great to place the fish there for a while, so that the fish skin browns and becomes crispy. Serve the oven vegetables on a platter and place the sea bass on top. Spoon some cooking liquid over the preparation and finish with chopped chives and/or parsley.

To prepare the gouda mash, peel the potatoes and boil them in water with a pinch of salt until it is tender. Drain and mash with a potato masher and add the butter, milk, egg yolk, good splash of fine olive oil, stirring in the gouda cheese. Adjust salt to taste. Serve the mash potatoes with a dash of olive oil or butter and freshly chopped parsley. Graag gedaaan! (You are welcome!)

SECTION 3

INTRODUCING NEW INGREDIENTS

★★★★★

"IT leaders' roles have evolved from managing internal IT operations to becoming co-creators of a digital future."

As the recipes in this Cookbook demonstrate conclusively, digital now runs through the core of successful private enterprises and public organisations. Master Chefs have seen their roles evolve rapidly during the past decade, from managing internal IT operations to becoming co-creators of a digital future. This evolution means that modern Master Chefs have dual but complementary responsibilities. They remain responsible for running stable and secure IT operations, but they are also accountable for providing guidance and tooling to support their peers in the execution of business strategies for the digital economy.

As we see in this section of the Cookbook, the starting point for digitisation at organisations such as Allianz Insurance and SPP—Sweden's first digital pensions company—is a digital platform that is secure, resilient, and scalable. Public cloud services and software-defined networks have replaced rigid and outdated private computing and communications facilities. The result of this transition is greater speed and agility. By migrating legacy applications to modern facilities, Master Chefs and their business partners discover new opportunities to connect with crucial data assets.

Our first playbook in this section, on "Next-Generation Infrastructure," vividly illustrates the steps that IT organisations need to take to achieve successful digital transformations. These steps include assessing the degree to which private facilities can be cloudified, choosing strategic partners and standards to support migration and acquiring internal skills to operate digital platforms in the new economy. We believe an additional goal for successful Master Chefs is to demonstrate how digital platforms can contribute to corporate sustainability goals.

This section makes it clear that cloud services have played a defining role in the transition to digital business, particularly in areas such as infrastructure modernisation, software development tooling, and the introduction of Software as a Service (SaaS). Master Chefs have shifted most applications to the cloud, although they retain a limited number of data centres for mission-critical workloads.

For Intel, data has become the key to corporate growth—both for itself and its clients. By connecting internal and external data sources together, decisions can be made faster, end-to-end processes can be streamlined for efficiency and effectiveness, and new commercial opportunities can be created. In every recipe in this section, the Master Chefs are creating data lakes to store and access the full complement of information assets. As Intel's Master Chef suggests: "Data is the glue that holds organisations together and fosters effective partnerships."

Both A2A—an Italian renewable energy group—and EasyJet are applying new technologies and toolsets to connect more closely with customers. In the case of A2A, IoT enables the company to monitor public spaces and domestic dwellings to improve the quality of the environment. EasyJet is reviewing new mobility techniques to offer travellers a seamless experience from home to destination.

But it's also important we raise a note of caution. The transition to multi-cloud services and hybrid work structures expands opportunities for attack and provides a new range of cyber-threat vectors. Since the start of the war in Ukraine, cyber criminals operating under rogue-state sponsorship are intensifying their efforts to disrupt operations, focusing on both infrastructures and data assets. Our playbook, "Managing the Escalating Cyber Risk," explores these threats and offers mediation strategies.

SIX
SECURE INFRASTRUCTURE

Traditional infrastructures that are based exclusively on private data centres and networks present significant hurdles for any company on its journey to digital business. Allianz Technologies identified the need to place integrated cloud platforms as the centre piece of its emerging digital insurance business. EasyJet, on other hand, recognised that its web-based reservation system had to be updated radically to suit today's sophisticated travellers.

Allianz's Master Chef has adopted five strategic initiatives around infrastructure renewal that enable its business units across the globe to respond to uncertain market conditions. The first of these initiatives is to stabilise and standardise underlying platforms to engender customer trust. Thereafter, these platforms can be modernised to take advantage of new techniques, such as software-defined networks and SaaS. These innovations help to delight customers and to attract the best talent.

The key benefits of cloud-based infrastructures are a combination of organisational agility, service innovation, and potential cost savings of up to 50%. In Allianz's experience, the move to cloud has established IT as a value contributor as well as an efficient service operator.

EasyJet changed the prevailing business model in the 1990s by adopting the web as the company's primary reservation channel. Systems and networks were designed around the web technologies of that time. Yet today's traveller is more reliant on mobile devices and expects a seamless journey from home to destination with no manual interventions. EasyJet's Master Chef is evaluating and deploying next-generation mobile applications, together with extensive cloud deployments, with the aim of outrunning aggressive start-ups. As part of this quest, sustainability has become a key tenet.

Allianz Technology

Delivering IT infrastructure for the future

Ingredients

- A bold, strategic plan helps transform legacy and fragmented technology solutions into a standard global multi-cloud platform
- Deployment of modern technologies, such as software-defined networks, deliver stable, secure, and cost-effective environment
- The client's interests must always be placed ahead of focusing on technological excellence alone

Preparing the dish

Natasha Davydova is Head of Infrastructure and Information Security at Allianz Technology, an operating entity of a major global insurance and asset management company Allianz SE. Having graduated with a degree in international economics and finance, she joined Accenture before moving into CIO and CTO positions with Standard Chartered and Deutsche Bank. Prior to joining Allianz Technology, Natasha was a senior executive with Salesforce.

Allianz SE, which is headquartered in Munich, has over 155,000 staff. The company is one of the world's largest insurers and is quoted on the Euro Stoxx 50 index. Allianz SE also operates under subsidiary brands in some countries, including Liverpool Victoria in the UK. Allianz Technology provides IT services to the operating entities that comprise Allianz SE globally. It employs over 12,000 people and growing, as the Group entities' IT operations are consolidated into Allianz Technology.

"Future Digital leaders should escape their comfort zones, keep learning, and be in constant touch with their customers in both good and challenging times."

Natasha Davydova, Head of Infrastructure and Information Security, Allianz Technology

Scan code to watch the full interview.

Adopting a five-point plan for technology

Allianz SE is part of a fast-moving sector that includes new InsurTech players operating in an uncertain economic environment. Customers seek personalised services that can be delivered anywhere at any time via multiple channels of their choice. Speed to market is critical, as well as flexible pricing that allows clients to pay for what they use. Natasha says Allianz Technology is using five strategic measures to respond to external pressures:

1. Enhancing stability and resilience of the underlying infrastructure and platforms that are vital to keeping customers satisfied and establishing an environment of trust. A "zero business impact outages" approach is essential to maintaining business continuity, as well as "zero trust" framework for comprehensive security coverage.
2. Providing organisational agility, so customers receive timely solutions precisely tailored to their business requirements. Agile development methods and minimum viable product techniques are essential to meeting customer expectations in a timely fashion.
3. Being the Employer of Choice in a war for talent. Allianz Technology seeks to attract and retain the best people by providing practical experiences that apply leading technology solutions to real use cases, as well as learning opportunities for employees to enhance their expertise and "future-proof" their skills.
4. Adopting new capabilities such as Software-Defined Wide Area Networks (SD-WAN) and SaaS, to scale up and standardise IT services across the globe.
5. Demonstrating commercial value from IT products and services that go beyond cost savings. Customer delight scores high on this scale, as does productivity improvement. This focus on business value has encouraged an emphasis on process mining, robotic process automation, AI, and machine learning.

Natasha's strategy within infrastructure and security is to accelerate digital transformation by implementing leading technology solutions and decommissioning legacy systems and technologies. For example, the main infrastructure initiatives include establishing a Future Cloud Platform to support cloud adoption and a global implementation of SD-WAN technology. Natasha is also focused on setting up a zero-trust security environment that moves protection from the perimeter to the individual information assets.

Future Cloud Platform

Natasha says cloud delivers tangible business benefits, including higher flexibility, lower maintenance costs, reduced dependency on legacy systems, and access to new channels. In the last several years Allianz Technology completed a successful consolidation of its data centres to achieve operational efficiency. To support Allianz Group's "Cloud First" strategy, Allianz Technology infrastructure team launched its Future Cloud Platform (FCP) initiative in 2019, with a team of 30 dedicated staff. FCP was set up with the objective to accelerate digital transformation across Allianz Group: building a true cloud culture and driving the transformation across Allianz technologies and operating entities.

FCP is the foundation enabling the customer application development teams to implement and host business applications in the public cloud based on Amazon Web Services and Microsoft Azure technologies. FCP is a key enabler of cloud transformation and a global Allianz standard for application hosting. However, it is not just a simple technical transformation of infrastructure; it also enables a modernization of legacy applications as part of the migration to the cloud. All major cloud services are consumed from the FCP. Natasha is not too concerned about vendor lock-in because she believes hyper-scalers are natural partners for innovation. For example, cloud providers are developing unique expertise around security, regulatory compliance, data platforms, and data management.

The FCP vision is to provide users an integrated, user-friendly, secure, and global public cloud platform so that they can build unique and state-of-the-art Allianz applications.

Implementing software-defined networks

Natasha's team has connected more than 1,700 offices via SD-WANs. This technology decouples traffic from traditional network structures and provides greater flexibility to operating entities. A combination of network virtualisation, cloudification, and automation significantly improved bandwidth to support business growth, strengthened security, and reduced costs by 30%.

Across the cloudification and network modernisation programmes, Natasha is keen to seek standard solutions for the Group. Shared services deliver economies of scale for the Allianz operating entities and ensure a stable and secure working environment.

Operating an effective IT kitchen

Natasha's team includes nearly 3,000 staff distributed across EMEA (Europe, Middle East, Africa), Americas and APAC (Asia-Pacific). Allianz Technology has a mandate to consolidate IT resources from the operating entities to achieve new economies of scale and scope.

Attracting and retaining talent is high on Natasha's agenda. She stresses the importance of work/life balance and diversity among her expanding team. She is building a culture of innovation and creativity and is keen to upskill her staff as mundane operational tasks are automated. Technology-led, customer-centric innovation is crucial in the competitive finance sector, and Allianz SE is proud of its award-winning blockchain-based solutions for claims processing.

Defining the qualities of a Master Chef

Clarity of vision, focus on results, and commitment to action have been the key success factors in Natasha's rapid career ascendancy. She encourages collaboration and trust within her team and promotes a blameless culture, where people learn from mistakes. Her philosophy is always to move forward.

Natasha aims to be client-focused at all times and to measure outcomes in terms of customer impact and satisfaction. Her clients are Allianz's operating entities across the globe. She is also keen to help contribute to society during what she describes as "the fifth industrial revolution," where corporates are expected to give back some of their wealth and expertise for the greater good for all.

As a Master Chef, Natasha passes on the attributes of trust, integrity and honesty to her team and family. She is mindful to choose her battles carefully. Natasha advises future digital leaders:

- To leverage disruptive technologies to encourage greater efficiency and automation, increase productivity, enhance customer insight, promote the development of superior products and services, and drive better decision making
- To use disruptive innovation not as a one-time investment, but rather as a continuing pledge to transform, develop and innovate
- To think beyond the old value chain to explore new ecosystems which digitally interconnect products, participants, and business models
- To expand beyond embracing today's best practices and lean into "future dynamic practices"—the tools, techniques and processes that encompass the emerging trends—such as design thinking, cognitive computing, and more

Natasha encourages future digital leaders to escape their comfort zone, to keep learning, and to be in constant touch with their customers in both good and challenging times.

EasyJet

Engineering seamless travel experiences

Ingredients

- Change and innovation are continuous processes, not one-off events
- Flexible platforms and resources will mitigate economic uncertainties
- CIOs should divide their time equally between the business and IT

Preparing the dish

Stuart Birrell is the CDO and CIO of EasyJet. He spends half his time managing IT and the other half managing the overall business. A graduate in electrical engineering from Heriot-Watt University with an MBA from Warwick, Stuart began his career building factories for Nissan Automotive. He progressed rapidly into IT with Kimberly-Clark and McLaren and later became CIO at Heathrow Airport. Two years ago, he joined EasyJet as a member of the executive committee.

EasyJet is a British multinational, low-cost airline group headquartered at Luton Airport and quoted on the London Stock Exchange. It operates domestic and international services on 927 routes in more than 34 countries. Founded in 1995, EasyJet employs 13,000 staff and flies more than 95 million passengers annually. The company started as a challenger to national airlines but was soon able to outstrip its rivals by appealing to low-cost travellers. It was the first airline to employ the Web as its primary reservation channel.

"Management maturity is about stepping out of your comfort zone while staying close to your best qualities."

Stuart Birrell, CDO and CIO, EasyJet

Scan code to watch the full interview.

Changing the business model

Despite its youth compared to national carriers, EasyJet needed to replace legacy systems that were 20-plus years old. Stuart was hired to help transform the business model by employing new IT platforms. Having already pioneered bookings over the Web, EasyJet faced fresh challenges from tech-driven start-up airlines. In Stuart's words: "There is no time to be complacent in this business." His earlier experiences at Heathrow provided a deep insight into the airline industry. This knowledge has enabled him to set a direction for the business as it seeks to beat new competition.

At the heart of Stuart's transformation is the replatforming of core systems, such as reservations, passenger services and yield management. This process has required an overhaul of the technology stack and a fresh approach to "make or buy" decisions. Stuart says low-cost airlines must lead in delivering operational efficiencies and offer constant innovations in customer experiences. EasyJet aims to create a seamless, end-to-end journey with no manual interventions.

Innovating the customer experience

Today, passengers moving through an airport might stop several times for security, luggage, and identity checks. In the future, technologies such as facial recognition should allow passengers to just "walk on board." Enabling this transition from current to future state requires new technological underpinnings and constant innovations to the booking and on-boarding processes. Stuart's team is responsible for setting enterprise standards but encourages IT and business staff to explore innovative solutions jointly.

Stuart does not believe in running a separate innovation team. Instead, he encourages his staff to try new things. Areas where innovation is critical include booking and yield management. The pandemic disrupted traditional demand patterns. Predicting passenger traffic is complex in the post-COVID age because of pent-up demand. EasyJet has used artificial intelligence to analyse internal and external data and generate new demand scenarios. The company is now working on next-generation mobile applications to improve customer experiences and fend off competitors.

Adopting new ways of operating

The EasyJet IT team consists of 250 internal staff and up to 400 external resources. Stuart focuses internal resources on what he believes is important to the business and leaves external parties to run day-to-day operations. However, he does draw on external expertise when none exists internally. He is careful to ensure everyone feels they're part of the team.

The task of supporting new business models, platforms, and products requires IT to evolve from a tight-knit organisation to one that is blended into the rest of the organisation. Stuart is keen for his team to share the latest techniques, such as Agile, with the business. He recognises IT must align its service support, platform, and application teams with the business to support its long-term aims. Stuart also understands that innovation is a constant work in progress, not a one-off event.

There have been major changes within IT to achieve business agility in an uncertain environment. EasyJet is now two-thirds of the way towards adopting public cloud, with test and development moving onto AWS and business functions adopting Software as a Service products. Cloud is the perfect solution to help manage the challenge of handling peak loads, such as the announcement of new routes creating a surge in demand.

Sustainability is a key business driver for EasyJet. Cloud enables carbon emissions to be scaled up or down carefully when compared to on-premises IT provision. The business devotes a great deal of effort to route optimisation to save fuel. Stuart predicts smaller aircraft of 100 seats will use sustainable fuel, such as hydrogen, by 2030. EasyJet is also committed to achieving carbon neutrality.

Defining the qualities of a Master Chef

Stuart says the role of the CIO has changed dramatically during the past decade. Historically, IT was a service to the business. Today, IT is the business. Stuart spends half his time looking after the wider interests of EasyJet, ranging from strategy to operational performance. He expects his C-suite peers to be tech-savvy. Successfully replatforming the business is the responsibility of all executive board members, not just IT.

Stuart sets direction for his IT organisation but does not labour the details. He proudly boasts about a two-page IT strategy that gives his team the freedom to pursue its own path. He believes the team should amplify his vision. Trust is crucial to this approach. However, Stuart is also impatient and drives his team hard towards results. He believes the ultimate success is when teams "self-actuate."

His advice to next-generation IT executives is to always seek help when they need it and find coaches and mentors to help them along the journey. He believes management maturity is about stepping out of your comfort zone while staying close to your best qualities.

Proper English Apple Strudel

Serves 4-6

- 800g or 4 Bramley apples, peeled, cored, sliced
- 100g golden granulated sugar
- Vanilla seeds scraped from 1 vanilla pod
- 2 tsp lemon juice and zest
- 35g each currant and sultanas
- 1 tsp ground allspice
- 1 tsp ground nutmeg
- 120g melted butter
- 6 large sheets filo pastry
- 1 Tbsp icing sugar for dusting
- 200ml English custard, ice cream or crème fraiche to serve

What makes this a proper English apple strudel is the use of the perfect English cooking apple—the Bramley. With one of the highest acidity levels of any apple, Bramley have the impeccable balance of sweetness and tartness and it quickly cooks down into the smoothest and lightest of apple purees, whilst retaining a rich sharp apple flavour.

Pre-heat oven to 200°C / 180°C fan / gas 6. Heat 100g of the sugar, 80g butter and the vanilla seeds in a medium, heavy-based frying pan over a medium-low heat for 5–8 minutes, or until golden brown and caramelised. Add the apples, lemon zest, currants, sultanas, allspice, and nutmeg, then cook for 10 minutes or until the apple is tender and smooth. Remove the apple mix from the pan and cool to room temperature.

Melt the rest of the butter in a pan. Place a clean tea towel on your kitchen worktop. Place a sheet of the filo on top, and brush with some of the melted butter and sprinkle over 1 tsp of sugar. Lay another sheet on top and repeat until you have used up all the 6 filo sheets. Now pile the apple filling generously on the filo, leaving a clear border all round. Tuck the ends in, then, using the tea towel to guide you, roll the pastry gently away from you to cover all the filling. Transfer the roll seam-side down to the lined baking sheet and brush with the rest of the melted butter. Bake for 40 to 45 minutes or until the whole house begins to smell heavenly and the pastry is golden brown and crisp.

Allow to cool to room temperature and dust with icing sugar. Cut each strudel into 6 diagonal slices. Serve slices each with a teeming dollop of crème fraiche, English custard, or Devonshire ice cream on top. Now that is the proper way to enjoy a good English dessert! This apple strudel can be made up to one day ahead and kept chilled to impress your dinning guests, that is if you can resist the temptation to not touch it.

The favourite dessert of Stuart Birrell

SEVEN
JOURNEY TO CLOUD

Digital is no longer confined to a limited number of sectors. During the past decade, digital has become pervasive, as demonstrated by two contrasting recipes in this subsection—one from RAI, Italy's state Radio and Television company, and another from SPP, Sweden's first digital pensions company.

RAI has pioneered the adoption of digital services such as content streaming and social media. This approach has enabled the company to maintain a television audience share of more than 40% in Italy. What's more, interactive services have enabled RAI to form an intimate relationship with its audience. RAI's Master Chef says digital platforms have played a pivotal role in transforming internal processes and external media services.

The company employs four different platforms to provide a solid foundation for its digital business. These include classical platforms to support internal processes and operating systems, as well as external platforms to link RAI to audiences and media agencies. The connectivity of data across RAI's four platforms is critical to its business success.

By undertaking a digital transformation journey, SPP has become a leader in both sustainable business practices and customer experiences. Under a radical programme of change known as the Future Core Programme, SPP's Master Chef examined every process and migrated 90% of the company's applications to the cloud. Cloud has opened the door to rapid product and service innovation, which helps SPP stay ahead of its competition.

Both Master Chefs recognise the central importance of modern cloud platforms as the mechanism to not just survive but to thrive in the emerging digital economy.

RAI

Building the digital foundations

> **Ingredients**
>
> - A multi-platform cloud foundation can support different parts of the business
> - A residual on-premises presence will help meet regulatory and business requirements
> - Leaders need the patience to accept what they can't change and the courage to change what they can

Preparing the dish

Massimo Rosso is ICT Director for RAI, Italy's public broadcasting service. With a first degree in theoretical physics and a master's degree in computer science, he acquired a deep knowledge of quantum mechanics early in his career, which has helped him track emerging technologies such as neural networks and quantum computing. Massimo joined RAI 30 years ago as a programmer and was appointed ICT Director in 2015. He is proud of his long tenure and is an active member of CIONET Italy's advisory board.

RAI, or Radiotelevision Italiana, is controlled by the Ministry of Economy and Finance. It runs a range of television and radio stations. In Italy, RAI has a high television audience share of more than 40%. Half its revenues come from licence fees and the remainder come from advertising. RAI is a member of the European Broadcasting Union.

Driving towards digital services

The media sector has been a pioneer in adopting digital services, such as content streaming and social media. RAI has been at the forefront of this digital transformation process. Massimo says the company has

"Curiosity and adaptability are essential ingredients for a successful technology career."

Massimo Rosso, ICT Director, RAI

Scan code to watch the full interview.

formed an intimate relationship with its audience during its digitisation journey. RAI's continuing efforts to deepen this relationship impact the culture and purpose of the organisation and demand a new, digital mindset.

As a successful multimedia group, RAI boasts wide variations in culture. In addition to skilled experts across programming and journalism, the organisation's capabilities also span functional departments, such as finance and procurement. Massimo believes staff across all departments should benefit from a common vision of digital, with shared values and objectives.

Massimo plays a pivotal role in helping RAI achieve this unifying goal. During his tenure, he has been influential in helping to transform internal processes and the external media services that are pushed to consumers. He has also improved underlying IT platforms. His relentless pursuit of digitisation has helped to reshape corporate mindsets beyond the boundaries of IT.

Building a digital foundation

Massimo says digital platform capability lies at the heart of RAI's transformation from broadcasting to interactive media services. The organisation has a proud heritage in IT, which started with the use of a central mainframe to capture and record details of individual subscribers in the 1960s.

Today, Massimo has moved most workloads and applications onto a multi-cloud environment. However, he has preserved two data centres in Rome and Turin to help RAI respond to the specialised demands of news services, and to ensure regulatory compliance and business continuity. Massimo has invested in four cloud platforms as part of the company's new digital foundations:

- Classical platforms that support internal processes and systems, such as SAP
- Platforms that manage physical assets, including modern sensor devices
- External platforms that link RAI to media-rating agencies and other utilities
- Platforms that give RAI a direct link to its audiences via the Web

The effective use of data across these digital platforms is crucial. For example, RAI uses predictive analytics to identify points of failure in its operational networks for broadcast and streaming. Massimo also runs business intelligence tools on top of cloud platforms to analyse audience behaviour. Another advantage of cloud computing is the ability to run neural networks, which enables artificial intelligence applications to be developed around a central data resource.

Positioning IT for a new digital era

Massimo says the IT organisation at RAI was traditionally focused on internal operations and process efficiencies. Today, IT plays a proactive role and develops new media products and services, as well as online customer channels. Technology continues to support new opportunities. Massimo believes fresh programme formats will emerge from the combination of edge computing and 5G.

Massimo's IT organisations includes 150 internal staff and 300 external collaborators. He has six senior managers, who he calls his "six pillars." They provide key functions, such as operational support, digital process design, engineering and architecture, and risk management. As the IT organisation continues to align ever-more closely with the business, Massimo's role is changing from operator to service integrator and service broker. His six managers are instrumental in affecting this transition.

Upskilling the IT workforce for digital business remains a significant challenge. Massimo is keen to attract a new generation of skilled staff from the best universities. However, he also recognises the importance of cohesion between existing staff and new employees, especially given generational age differences. Massimo's approach is to build trust and offer opportunities to new joiners. He believes his new IT organisation is designed to support a multi-generational workforce.

Defining the qualities of a Master Chef

Massimo recognises IT leadership has become more complex due to a multiplicity of technologies associated with the rise of digital business. He uses storytelling techniques to place change within a historic perspective. He believes a technology-driven culture is about producing quantifiable results, but communications should embody purpose to drive a positive emotional response.

Massimo believes successful Master Chefs recognise that self-awareness is crucial for mastering complex situations. To boost his skills in this area, Massimo studies subjects outside IT, including philosophy and sociology. He derives inspiration from his grandfather, who believed broader horizons lie within the individual rather than outside.

When it comes to managing his senior team, Massimo adopts a three-stage approach to decision-making processes. First, he encourages all team members to share their ideas in free flow. Second, he requires the team to close the gap between the desirable and the practical. Finally, he looks for actionable programmes that can deliver clear outcomes.

Massimo's advice to aspiring digital leaders is to "follow your patience." He says everyone should recognise the future is not yet written, so curiosity and adaptability are essential ingredients for a successful technology career.

SPP

Becoming a digital front-runner in financial services

> **Ingredients**
>
> - "Digital" opens a new world of possibilities in a crowded marketplace
> - Agile rather than waterfall is the best way to deliver transformation
> - A career is a marathon, not a sprint, and patience is a virtue along the way

Placing the dish

Kristin Lindmark joined Accenture in 2000 and spent eight years managing large international projects in financial services. Kristin then worked at If Insurance for three years. She joined SPP, one of the leading pension providers in Sweden, in 2011, becoming CIO in 2013. She joined telecommunications firm Telenor Sweden as CIO in November 2021.

SPP provides insurance products for companies, organisations, and private individuals. SPP is part of the Storebrand Group. The Storebrand Group has roots dating back to 1767 and is a leading provider in the Nordic market for pensions, life and health insurance, banking, and asset management.

Introducing the Future Core Programme

SPP encountered shrinking margins in 2015. The firm faced a combination of market pressures externally and a fragmented application landscape internally. Sweden had also become a favoured target for newly emerging InsurTech companies. SPP recognised incremental improvements would not address this range of existential challenges. In 2016, the board voted for a radical change programme, known as the Future Core Programme, that would transform SPP into a front-runner as a digital pensions company in Sweden.

With Future Core, SPP shifted its entire operational platform with a standard system as their new core system, enabling new digital solutions and migrating from old legacy applications to one core system. This process required the decommissioning of legacy systems, many of which dated back to the 1980s. By 2021, SPP had migrated 95% of the policies and created yearly savings of €5 million. Maintaining continuity and ensuring that new development could be released in parallel with the migration journey during this period was a key challenge. The migration was extremely complex with contracts lasting up to 50 years with both its business and consumer clients.

The project was a catalyst for change for SPP. In Future Core, SPP examined every process inside and outside, developing new ways-of-work. Kristin says running this huge transformation programme was comparable to undertaking a heart transplant while the patient was up and running.

Earning prizes for success

The investment paid off and in 2019, SPP won an award at CIO awards for having the first fully digital pension offering in Sweden. It was also recognised as a leading proponent of sustainable business practices, having eliminated paper from its operations.

The number one benefit of the transformation programme was the system rationalisation that created simplicity with a more efficient, automated operational platform, enabling new digital services to be built.

A second key benefit of the programme has been the ability to work seamlessly with distribution partners. Small companies with digital business models are eager to join forces with larger, more established firms across the insurance ecosystem. Digitisation has created new opportunities for product and service innovation at SPP that would be impossible in a traditional insurance business.

Modernising the kitchen

The 70 IT staff at SPP were divided into two domains—core and digital. The core team looks after infrastructure and enterprise applications. The digital team provides innovative services to the business across areas such as UX design, data analytics, and technology enablement.

Agile methodologies have been key to delivering the Future Core Programme. Initially, SPP chose to adopt a waterfall approach to application modernisation. However, this was incompatible with the company's desire to move quickly and enable it to deliver business value in parallel

"A career is a marathon, not a sprint."

Kristin Lindmark, CIO, SPP

Scan code to watch the full interview.

with the large migration initiative. Agile was adopted across IT and the rest of the business to help accelerate change and overcome bottlenecks. SPP implemented a single pipeline for ongoing projects that gave the company greater visibility and control over the change programme.

As with many reengineering programmes, emotions ran high in the early stages of the programme. However, SPP and its staff stayed courageous, and a can-do attitude developed among the workforce. The organisation is now working closely together and has matured its Agile work with a range of smooth-running processes.

Redefining the role of the kitchen

Kristin developed new insights into IT management during her many years of transformation at SPP. She describes the journey as "building a digital cathedral rather than crafting new stones." The Future Core Programme has elevated IT strategy to the centre of the company's business strategy.

IT now has two distinct roles. First, creating a stable and secure operating environment, which is crucial for any financial services company. Second, enabling the business to create new pockets of value in its investment strategy, which helps strengthen relationships with partners and customers.

The speed of change in the insurance industry means SPP must spot and respond to trends rapidly, and for that you need an organisation and an application landscape that is prepared for rapid change. The company understands that the future is uncertain. SPP must formulate a strong vision and take small but decisive steps towards its end goal.

Defining the qualities of a Master Chef

Kristin says effective digital leadership is all about storytelling. She used the Future Core Programme as a metaphor on how to become a front-runner by taking small steps. The story captured the attention of the market and raised the level of confidence of the organisation. Kristin recognises Stockholm is home to many digital natives, so she told her story to help attract talent and maintain a top team within the digital kitchen.

Sustainability is a foundational focus area within the Storebrand Group and influenced how Kristin managed her IT organisation at SPP. SPP adopted a strict approach to IT sourcing, cloud platforming, and business travel, which exemplified how IT plays a key role in reaching net-zero outcomes. Kristin is also a champion of diversity—45% of her staff at SPP were female.

Her advice to next-generation CIOs is to grab opportunities and seek the requisite skills to thrive in a digital economy. She emphasises that patience is a virtue: "A career is a marathon, not a sprint.

Kristin left SPP to become CIO at Telenor in November 2021.

Thai Mango Sticky Rice

Serves 4

- 1 to 2 ripe mangoes
- 1 cup Thai sweet rice (Glutinous or sticky rice)
- 120g water
- 400ml or 1 can full creamed coconut milk
- ¼ teaspoon salt
- 4 to 5 Tbsp brown, palm or cane sugar, to taste

This celebrated heavenly Thai dessert known as khao niaow ma muang needs no introduction as it is well-known throughout Southeast Asia and the rest of the world. Famously served as street food in Thailand, this dessert is usually eaten during the peak mango season in April and May and can be served either hot or cold. The taste of this tropical sweet rice pudding dessert is tantalising, irresistible, and moreish. The good news is that it is also very easy to make at home.

This mango sticky rice recipe requires only a few key ingredients. The choice of the type and ripeness of the mango is key. Use the sweetest and ripest mango you can find and use only the best quality coconut cream or full cream coconut milk for the rice pudding. Ideally, you need a rice cooker to make the sticky rice, but you can also use a pot on your stove to make the prefect sticky rice.

Let's start by soaking the rice in 1 cup of water in a heavy based pot for 20 to 30 minutes. Do not drain the rice. Add ½ cup more water and tip in half the can of the coconut milk or cream. Add a pinch of salt and 1 tablespoon of the brown/palm/cane sugar. Stir well. Bring to a gentle boil, then partially cover with a lid (leaving some room for steam to escape). Reduce heat to medium-low, or just until you get a gentle simmer. Simmer for another 20 to 30 minutes, or until the coconut water has been fully absorbed by the sticky rice. Turn off the heat but leave the pot on the burner with the lid on tight. Allow it to sit for 5 to 10 minutes.

To make the delightful coconut sauce, warm—but make sure not to boil—the remaining coconut milk over medium-low heat in a small saucepan for about 5 to 8 minutes. Add 3 tablespoons brown, palm, or cane sugar, stirring it together to dissolve. Taste and adjust the sweetness of the sauce and add more sugar if you like it sweeter. Prepare the mangoes by cutting them open and slicing them into bite-sized pieces or wedges.

When everything's ready, scoop the exquisite warm rice into a serving bowl, drizzle it with the sweet coconut sauce, arrange the mango slices on top or on the side, and then smother it with more coconut sauce so that the rice is almost swimming in this thick lustrous cream. Take a bite and be instantly transported to a sunny white sandy beach in Thailand!.

The favourite dessert of Michal Paprocki

EIGHT
DATA

The two recipes in this subsection emphasise the central role of data in two organisations—Intel, a global leader in chip manufacturing, and A2A, an Italian company that generates, distributes, and markets renewable energy. These two recipes illustrate clearly how data-centric business models enable revenue growth and operational efficiencies.

Intel recognises that data is a critical weapon in the digital economy. With about 80 zettabytes (that's 80 x 10^{21} bytes) of data generated globally every year, the challenge is for digital leaders to ingest and analyse the huge volumes of information their businesses collect for commercial purposes. Intel's Master Chef advises digital leaders to harness the data that is readily available by using advanced techniques such as artificial intelligence and analytics, and to liberate data that is hidden in legacy systems.

It's also important to recognise that the task of harnessing data effectively presents digital leaders with new challenges, as volumes of information continue to expand, and disruptive technologies emerge. Intel's Master Chef says digital leaders should stay open to new ideas and should be ready to take advantage of Web 3.0 and blockchain developments as they mature.

A2A has a 10-year plan to double its current revenues and profits. The company is keen to address new markets and geographies and to use sensing technologies and 5G connectivity to monitor homes, public spaces, and smart buildings. By combining these technologies with AI and analytics, A2A can help citizens and local authorities reduce air pollution and generate advanced flood warnings. At the same time, A2A recognises the power that data holds in providing predictive maintenance and capacity planning within its internal operations.

In both recipes, the adoption of open architectures and cloud platforms helps the businesses harness and connect ever-growing volumes of data.

A2A S.p.A

Adopting a tri-modal approach to digital and sustainability

Ingredients

- New business horizons associated with sustainability must be recognized and navigated
- The existing factory can be modernised by placing digital at the core of operations
- Current operations can act as a business incubator for new revenue-generating possibilities

Preparing the dish

Marco Moretti is the Group CIO of A2A S.p.A. With a degree in IT science and mathematics, Marco spent 12 years at Accenture, where he developed a strong focus on client issues in the energy sector. He then joined Gaz de France, which merged with Suez in 2008 to form Engie. In 2015, he joined A2A, motivated by its aim to double revenues and profits in renewable energy and utilities.

A2A is an Italian company that generates, distributes, and markets renewable energy, electricity, gas, integrated water supplies, and waste management. A2A was born from the merger of two city-owned companies, AEM and ASM, at the end of 2007. It is still partially owned by the municipalities of Milan and Brescia.

Responding to the sustainability agenda

With a recognition of the significant opportunities associated with the production of renewable energies and the broader sustainability agenda, A2A has developed a 10-year strategy to double its current revenues of €7 billion and its profits of €1.2 billion. The strategy is based around three pillars:

"Delivery must take place bottom-up rather than top-down to ensure inclusivity across the workforce."

Marco Moretti, Group CIO, A2A

Scan code to watch the full interview.

- Expanding A2A's footprint from its home country to cover the entire European region
- Focusing on renewables of all kinds, including wind and solar energies
- Exploiting the circular economy to identify where reuse of waste products is possible

Marco and his board recognise digital sits at the centre of this strategy, and they know the role of the CIO and IT organisation is pivotal to delivering stretched business outcomes. Half of the total €2.8 billion earmarked to achieve the company's 10-year goals relates to digital technologies.

How IT will help deliver a digital vision

Working to this stretched, decade-long target requires both a multiplicity of changes to the core business and a series of new, break-out developments. To help deliver IT that supports A2A's three strategic pillars, Marco has mobilised four major programmes within his IT organisation to reshape the existing business.

The first is to develop digital twins of all physical assets within the group. By harnessing data in these twins, the business can adopt a predictive approach to maintenance and capacity planning. This approach will help prevent supply disruption but can also be used to optimise capacity to meet business growth and fluctuations in customer demand. The second programme is geared towards process efficiency. A2A wants to avoid the linear expansion of its workforce as it aims to double its revenues. Automation can help introduce a "non-linear" expansion of labour.

These first two programmes are underpinned by a requirement to develop scalable and adaptive digital platforms that support modern applications. Marco recognises that heritage systems will need to be replaced in the coming years to support new services. He is using Platform as a Service (PaaS) technologies to modernise applications. He also emphasises the need for open systems to encourage vendor and industry partnerships.

The third programme addresses how A2A will reach six million customers in the future, which compares to three million today. This growth will require the wholesale digitisation of customer channels and the use of robotic process automation to reduce the load on frontline staff. The final component of the digital programme focuses on employees, a large proportion of whom remain embedded in the analogue world.

Marco is working actively with HR to ensure all staff feel comfortable to transition to a fully digital organisation.

Developing break-out options

Alongside the modernisation of existing operations, Marco is eager to combine new business models and technologies, such as the Internet of Things (IoT), to transform how cities will be managed in the future. Marco believed the potential of these developments merited a brand-new start-up to achieve leadership in key areas, including the metering of all utilities at home and across parks and byways. The combination of IoT and 5G produces low cost, low-power devices that are capable of providing new functionalities for smart metres and video input.

Marco organised five hackathons to develop the concept of the smart city. This initiative generated more than 30 new services for areas such as flood and air-pollution monitoring. Marco recognised smart buildings could help track and reduce energy use dramatically. Many more applications are emerging, including systems that boost security in public places and help schedule recharge stations.

These start-ups highlight how CIOs and IT organisations can act as an incubator. By working outside the main business, Marco can seed new opportunities and decide quickly whether these businesses will fail or scale. Ultimately, successful start-ups can be incorporated back into the main business.

Building a world-class digital kitchen

Marco has a staff of 140 working directly for him at the corporate centre. These staff are mirrored across four main business units. As the digital coordinator, Marco believes IT can deliver 10% of tomorrow's profit. He believes IT operates in a "tri-modal" fashion with the following characteristics:

- Delivering operational resilience through best-in-breed platforms and partnerships
- Reengineering critical processes by employing appropriate methods and tools
- Being a business innovator by providing an incubator for start-up businesses

Defining the role of a Master Chef

Marco recognises the failure rate of large IT programmes can exceed 70%. He is the coordinator of digital transformation but not the primary lead. Successful digital transformation requires strong executive partnerships. He believes every part of the business, such as finance, sales, and HR, must work together to achieve transformational outcomes. Marco thinks of himself as a chief innovation and coordination officer. Strong central governance is key across new areas of the business. However, delivery must take place bottom-up rather than top-down to ensure inclusivity across the workforce.

Marco believes effective leadership is about being transparent and open. His advice to next-generation CIOs is to recognise that digital will "flood" their organisations. They should see themselves as principal actors in the emerging digital economy.

Marco Moretti left A2A S.p.A. to become the Digital Transformation Director at the Agenzia per la Cybersicurezza Nazionale in Nov 2022.

Intel

Innovating at the core of the digital economy

Ingredients

- An open foundation is the cornerstone of successful ecosystems
- The new commercial imperative involves connecting and analysing data
- Staff need to be empowered to innovate in a continuous fashion

Preparing the dish

Melissa Evers is Vice President of the software and advanced technology group and General Manager of the strategy and execution team at Intel. After acquiring a degree in engineering and an MBA from the University of Texas, her career evolved in three chapters. She worked initially as a field engineer at Exxon Mobil, then progressed to strategy and finance at Dell, and in 2004, took up a senior post at Intel to focus on software development. She is proud of her current employer and its remarkable heritage. In her words, Intel put the "silicon" into Silicon Valley.

Intel is the world's largest semiconductor manufacturer by revenue and is one of the developers of the x86 series of instruction sets that can be found in most personal computers (PCs). The firm was founded in 1968 by Gordon Moore and Robert Noyce. Intel's investment in microprocesses in the 1990s fostered the rapid growth of the PC. The company has demonstrated constant innovation in areas beyond the PC, including Wi-Fi and software-defined networks. Intel has become a standard-bearer for open standards along with Red Hat.

Competing in the digital economy

All business leaders recognise the importance of data in the digital economy. We generate around 80 zettabytes of data annually, with projections of 180 zettabytes by 2025. Melissa says ubiquitous computing lies at the heart of the digital economy and has fuelled this rapid increase in data. She says the key challenge for business today is to ingest and analyse vast quantities of structured and unstructured data through new techniques, including artificial intelligence and advanced analytics. Melissa says compute power is the foundation stone that converts data into value.

Computing power has evolved rapidly into every aspect of today's economy, from software-defined networks to edge computing and onto cloud platforms. Microprocesses permeate every layer of the technology stack, from basic connectivity such as IoT to higher levels of intelligence that are powered by AI. Melissa's team works with technology partners—such as Red Hat and its enterprise customers—to ensure that the software embedded in Intel's hardware can add value across the stack.

Harnessing the data

Melissa says harnessing vast quantities of data requires two approaches. The first is to take advantage of what you already have. Here, she mentions techniques such as business intelligence, data-streaming services, and automation. These tools increase the quality of existing data and add value to product design and customer experiences. However, she provides a cautionary note. You can only add value if data is connected, which relies on open standards and architectures.

The second approach is to harness what Melissa refers to as "dark data," which is information stored in legacy systems and applications. Dark data is unlikely to be standardised or connected. It can be scattered across geographies and operating units. Most corporates recognise that converting dark data into value requires wholescale modernisation of the IT estate, including the migration of legacy apps to the cloud. Modern cloud infrastructures provide the connectivity and tooling to enable easy access to data sources.

Envisaging a new technological landscape

Once data is accessible and, amenable to powerful analytic tools, businesses can adopt new

"Becoming a successful manager is like breaking out of the chrysalis. It requires a change of behaviour from rigidity to flexibility."

Melissa Evers, Vice President of the software and advanced technology group and General Manager of the strategy and execution team, Intel

Scan code to watch the full interview.

ways of working. There is much evidence that data-centric business models generate value. We only need to look at digital natives, such as Google, Amazon, and Netflix, to see the economic impact of such models. Entirely new industries have emerged during the past 20 years, including Software as a Service provisions and content streaming, which illustrate the value of data-centric approaches.

Melissa also sees opportunity arising from disruptive trends, such as Web 3.0, cryptocurrencies, blockchain, and cybersecurity. She is optimistic that corporations such as Intel will be able to exploit these disruptions and solve critical global challenges, including climate change and future pandemics. From her experiences, data will be key to unlocking the answers to these challenges.

Melissa also believes collaboration between members of the ecosystem will be crucial to driving neutral, horizontal innovation. She gives the example of the strategic partnership between Intel and Red Hat. Both parties have promoted open standards that encompass operating systems such as Linux and advanced infrastructures such as software-defined networks. These standards and infrastructures provide an open platform on which innovation takes place.

Fostering innovation within Intel

Intel is universally recognised as one of Silicon Valley's most innovative companies. Nevertheless, Melissa recognises that maintaining sustained innovation is challenging in an organisation with 100,000 employees. Intel has institutionalised innovation through its labs, but it also expects every employee to contribute to this endeavour. The 15,000 engineers who work most closely with customers and business partners are empowered to innovate through a flat organisational structure.

Melissa is keen to encourage her engineers to take risks and learn from their mistakes. Being a good listener is essential in organisational learning. Successes must be celebrated and individuals rewarded. Collaboration with external parties is critical to scaling innovation and boosting shareholder value.

Defining the qualities of a Master Chef

Melissa uses a colourful metaphor to describe her journey from individual contributor to senior manager. She refers to the evolution of a butterfly from caterpillar to a chrysalis and into a beautiful flying insect. She says becoming a successful manager is like breaking out of the chrysalis. It requires a change of behaviour from rigidity to flexibility.

As a passionate and energetic person, Melissa looks for the best in every individual she manages. She emphasises the need to overcome fear and intimidation in an elevated community by referring to the advice of her father: "Everyone puts their pants on one leg at a time."

Melissa advises aspiring Master Chefs to make our planet a better place by constantly looking for problems to solve and applying innovative solutions. She says everyone should adopt a beginner's mindset.

PLAYBOOK 6

MANAGING THE ESCALATING CYBER RISK

Digital leaders must ensure boards know the potential for damage and the importance of measures that can mitigate the danger

The move to hybrid working and multi-cloud services has expanded the range of cyber-threat vectors dramatically. Recent developments around the globe—most notably the invasion of Ukraine by Russia, plus massive macro-economic instability—have further exacerbated the potential for cybersecurity incidents that put businesses, their employees, and their customers at risk.

Cyber criminals and nation-state actors with errant aims have intensified their efforts to disrupt corporations and damage critical infrastructures. As attacks become more frequent, legacy approaches—such as simply relying on an enterprise firewall—might fail to meet the current and ever-increasing security challenges that organisations face. It is time to re-evaluate cyber defences.

Who are the bad actors?

Nation-state actors, such as Russia, Iran, North Korea, and China, have always held a strong position on the frontline of cyberattacks. As state-funded operations, these actors have access to the most sophisticated tools and are also able to innovate at a rapid pace.

What's already clear is that continuing global instabilities have fuelled higher levels of attacks in recent months, especially from Russia and China. All the evidence from the research community is that the situation is likely to get worse. A combination of war, inflation, and recession will encourage more criminal activity at home as well as abroad.

The good news, however, is that the cyber-defence sector continues to learn more about these threat actors and their techniques every day. Specialist cyber-technology providers are building ever-more powerful capabilities, such as zero-trust platforms, with careful attention paid to identity management and security.

A zero-trust model is an approach to the design and implementation of security systems that says businesses should trust no one. Zero-trust security relies on verification. Devices should not be trusted by default and multi-factor authentication should be deployed.

Digital leaders should also pay close attention to the emergence of new technology. In the coming years, we can expect that quantum computing-powered tools will be deployed by state actors in their ongoing attempts to break every conceivable defence that is created by providers and implemented by businesses.

Just as bad actors continue to search for new techniques to break enterprise systems, so the supply side and the customers that use their technology solutions must focus on innovation in an attempt to stay at least one step ahead of the aggressors.

Do boards take the escalating cyber risk seriously enough?

CIONET has spoken with a range of digital leaders about their experiences when it comes to explaining the escalating cyber risk to boards. The general feeling is that cyber itself does not resonate well with non-technical peers; instead, only the broader aspects of risk mitigation are up for discussion.

Other CIOs have talked to us about the need to include both IT and cyber in the corporate risk register. Taking this approach requires a careful quantification of risks to the business and a detailed set of risk-mitigation procedures. While both of these measures are possible, it's also the case that not all sectors—or even organisations—have achieved this status today.

It's also important to recognise that budgets for cyber defences vary widely between different industries. For example, financial services firms regularly spend as much as 20% of their IT budget on security measures.

At a more general level, there is a perception amongst CIOs that boards recognise that many elements of the modern world have become extremely volatile. The war in Ukraine, and its resulting disruptive impact on global supply chains, is damaging business confidence. In such a fast-changing global situation, business resilience is a key imperative for every organisation.

One thing is certain in an age of uncertainty: all kinds of cyberattacks will continue to occur. Businesses and their employees must be prepared to respond quickly to reduce the potential impact of an attack on their day-to-day operational activities.

All CIOs recognise that tighter governance measures will be required to help their organisations defend against potential cyberattacks. One digital leader has suggested that CISOs should receive specialist communications training, so they can become storytellers rather than technical analysts. The explanation is simple: boards respond well to stories, even if they touch on technicalities.

How do changes in the IT landscape affect information security?

CIOs and their C-suite peers must also recognise that the outsider threat is not the only element that might lead to an impact on IT security. CIONET members have provided many examples of digital transformations taking place within

IT organisations and how these changes could potentially leave the door open for higher-level attacks. These examples include:

- A move to multi-cloud environments, which expands attack surfaces and complicates traditional defence measures, such as antivirus and firewalls
- A shift to an enterprise data lake as a single source of truth can actually simplify unauthorized access to corporate data compared to when fragmented assets are locked away in legacy systems
- A migration of applications from legacy systems—which are often inert to attacks—to cloud native applications can mean that networked resources are now vulnerable
- A growing use of shadow IT practices amongst employees can lead to people deploying Software as a Service applications in front- and back-office scenarios without the knowledge of the technology organisation

CIOs believe that many of these additional risk factors can be addressed by tighter governance. At the design stage, procedures such as DevSecOps—which involves introducing security earlier in the software development life cycle—can help to build security practices and processes into new applications, reducing both design costs and the chances of an attack.

In addition, a move by some organisations to integrated or more centralised IT governance can also help to reduce vulnerabilities through the imposition of standardised frameworks. Government organisations seem to be well placed in this regard, through a combination of support from the UK's National Cyber Security Centre, the GCHQ intelligence service, and specialist frameworks that are being promoted by the Cabinet Office.

What are the practical measures that businesses can adopt?

All CIOs accept that it's impossible to reduce the risk of attack to zero. However, strong defences create a significant impediment to bad actors. Organisations must seek to understand and quantify the risk of cyberattacks and should take advice from regulators to stay within acceptable guidelines.

One CIO has stressed to CIONET the need to build detailed inventories of IT assets, such as software, hardware, and data. By knowing what you have, risk mitigation becomes more of a science than an art.

Next steps for CISOs, CIOs and CTOs

While the cyber risk continues to escalate, digital leaders who contributed to our research suggest a number of measures that can be taken now to help reduce the threat to business:

- Accept that attacks will happen and that appropriate procedures must be in place to reduce their impact. These measures must cover all aspect of a business, including its people, processes, and the development of the cultural acceptance of risk.
- Build security into every aspect of the evolving IT landscape, from cloud migration to changing vendor relationships. DevSecOps will play an important role in this work.
- Adopt zero-trust security as your overall platform, with associated multi-authentication techniques covering identity management.
- Ensure that your board is fully conversant with the range of cyber risks and that they understand how they have the ultimate responsibility for its impact on the business.

PLAYBOOK 7

NEXT-GENERATION INFRASTRUCTURE: CLOUDED IN UNCERTAINTY

To help their businesses embrace the rapid pace of change, digital leaders must focus on building next-generation infrastructures now

We are living through a period of unprecedented technology-enabled change. Business cycles have been compressed from years or decades to weeks and days. The most visible example of this shift came in spring 2020, when the world's biggest companies transferred hundreds of thousands of workers from offices to homes. What might once have been an intractable challenge was completed quickly and successfully.

One technology above all others is the enabler: cloud computing. Ground-level developments in cloud technologies, such as Infrastructure as a Service (IaaS) and Platform as a Service (PaaS), have provided the foundations for businesses to shift their businesses models. On top of this cloud-enabled base, companies have adopted Software as a Service (SaaS) applications to transform how employees and customers access services over the web. CIOs and CTOs are at the centre of this seismic shift.

Understanding the shift to the cloud

Digital leaders who are charged with managing the cloud-enabled businesses of today face a very different landscape to the one they encountered in the past. In the traditional model of IT management, the IT chief's role was relatively straightforward: negotiate better deals with outsourcing partners for the primary towers: data centres, networks, and end-user computing.

Today, the traditional model of IT management looks tired and stale. Most organisations are taking steps towards a hybrid mix of on-premises, private, and public cloud. While some companies are further along in their journey than others, evidence suggests there's no business strategy without a cloud strategy.

However, the destination is a long way in the distance. Yes, public cloud delivers the agility to cope with periods of rapid change and uncertainty, but these services are at a nascent stage of development. Estimates suggest the public cloud accounts for just 10% of what IT services spend. Many barriers litter the pathway to a comprehensive adoption of public cloud services, including a migration from legacy applications, an investment in ageing hardware, and a lack of appropriate skills.

Cloud will begin to dominate by 2027

Yet, we believe it is conceivable that between 50% and 60% of workloads could shift to flexible and Agile public cloud platforms by 2027. Within three to five years, many of the legacy applications that populate on-premises systems will have been redeveloped to become cloud-native, using Agile methods and DevOps techniques. Other developments that could contribute to this shift include:

- Growing demand for high-performance computing (HPC) to solve complex problems
- Consolidation of corporate data from separate applications to a single data lake
- Emergence of industry clouds that reflect the growing need to share data

Compute and storage are becoming global utilities, where the scale and geographic coverage boasted by the dominant players creates high barriers to newcomers. In the SaaS market space, a growing number of players hold niche positions in the public cloud, such as Salesforce for CRM and Zscaler for security. CIOs and CTOs will need to work with service integrators to find the best solutions for their compute environments.

An endpoint for next-generation infrastructures

Our ongoing research with the CIONET member community indicates that a cloud-first strategy should include the following components:

- Transfer of hardware ownership (CAPEX) to a pay-as-you-go (OPEX) model—this merits a move to public cloud for all IaaS. Cloud will provide the necessary agility and flexibility to cope with uncertain demand patterns.
- Adoption of software-defined networks—these architectures will enable companies to dispense with older infrastructures. Automation, including artificial intelligence and robotic process automation, will help optimise and manage such facilities.
- Migration of corporate applications to a cloud-native environment—this will rely heavily on Agile methods and DevOps techniques to speed up the re-platforming process. Companies will choose to exploit PaaS to take advantage of embedded tools.
- Consolidation of data assets—this will require embedded databases to be transported into virtual data lakes within public clouds. RPA and AI will help to accelerate this migration by locating, cleansing, and standardising data.
- Securing a multi-cloud infrastructure—having transported corporate data and applications to public clouds, organisations will need to operate boundary-less perimeters. This is already the case with many external services, such as SaaS. Zero Trust regimes will also be required.

So, how can organisations create a successful cloud-first strategy? In the case of digital natives, the answer has been to adopt microservices to support changes to front-end commercial products and services. The success of this loosely coupled approach means many IT organisations—not just digital natives—are now considering new architectures based on microservices.

For some digital leaders at slow-moving corporates, this new organisation might appear a long way in the distance. However, there is no room for complacency. Just as Web 3.0, blockchain and decentralised architectures are approaching on the horizon, the adoption of microservices is an inevitable consequence of the fast-emerging digital economy.

Assessing the magnitude and direction of change

The starting point in any major transition to a future position is an assessment of the current state. Having created a baseline, it is feasible to start plotting a roadmap to the envisaged end state and to develop a detailed design that is ready to be implemented. The key factors to be considered are:

- Ownership and configuration of private networks and data centres—most organisations, especially in financial services, will need to preserve a small number of strategic data centres to house mission-critical applications. These might require limited private network facilities.
- Assessing legacy applications for cloud readiness—CIOs and CTOs will need to document and assess which of the many hundreds of on-premises applications can be migrated into the cloud, either by a "lift and shift" or full conversion to cloud-native formats.
- Choosing strategic partners and associated standards—with the decline of traditional outsourcing contracts, CIOs and CTOs will need to consider who will be the most appropriate platform and service partners to support a hybrid structure.
- Reskilling the IT organisation—the adoption of Agile methods and DevOps will require a new generation of skilled programmers and business analysts. CIOs and CTOs will need to collaborate closely with the businesses to deliver value-based outcomes.
- Meeting sustainability goals—CEOs have been vocal in declaring their commitment to net-zero targets by 2030. IT needs to be a contributor to achieving such targets. IT can also provide many of the tools to assist other parts of the organisation in this endeavour.

We believe these factors in combination require a comprehensive transformation of not only the infrastructure but the entire IT organisation itself.

Adopting a next-generation mindset

The global environment today presents unprecedented levels of change and uncertainty. The pace of change has increased dramatically in recent years due partly to the pandemic, macro-economic turmoil, and geopolitical instability, but also new waves of technology, including blockchain, 5G, IoT, AI, and VR. The pace of change is only likely to accelerate.

Digital leaders will play a central role in helping their organisations adjust to this new velocity. Here are some ways in which CIOs and CTOs can help:

- Offer techniques that are appropriate to high levels of uncertainty, such as scenario planning. For example, consider how new waves of technology-led innovation will have a profound effect on future business landscapes.
- Provide education and guidance on how digital technologies and processes can address business problems in a new and fundamental manner.

This approach requires full participation by IT leadership in all aspects of business planning and operations.

- Build and run cloud-based platforms that can support digital business models. Such platforms should encourage experimentation and hyper-scaling of new concepts (build the new), as well as the transformation of existing operations (modernise the factory).

Dealing with this level of change will not be straightforward, yet IT has several advantages over other functions. First, it is frequently the channel through which new, innovative ideas enter an organisation. Second, it reaches into every aspect of a business, both at the front and back end.

By designing and implementing next-generation digital infrastructures, IT can provide the foundations on which organisations evolve and flourish.

Next steps for CIO and CTOs

Digital leaders must focus on next-generation infrastructures now. Decade-long arrangements, characterised by rigid outsourcing contracts, are being replaced by flexible public cloud relationships. By mid-decade, it is likely that large organisations will achieve a balance for their provision: one-third each for on-premises, private, and public cloud.

The transition to a next-generation infrastructure is a genuine business transformation. It will require different skills, tools, and partnerships that didn't exist in previous generations. Our research suggests organisations are instituting these actions:

- Assessment of current infrastructures, such as asset inventories, external contracts, and traffic-pattern analysis
- Design of an endpoint vision for next-generation infrastructures that embraces the need for flexibility and agility
- Development of a practical route map for the implementation of new designs, including strategic partnerships, skills, and tooling
- Construction of a business case that aligns infrastructure refresh with broader commercial goals, where infrastructure is a value-enabler rather than merely a cost

Cup of Baklava Delight

Serves 20 cookies

Pastry Dough

- 85g cream cheese, softened
- 120g butter, softened
- 42g almond flour
- 42g coconut flour
- 42g ground golden flaxseed
- 1 egg yolk

Nut Filling

- 96g chopped nuts (pistachios, walnuts, almonds or pecan)
- 50g butter
- ½ tsp cinnamon
- ⅓ tsp cardamon powder

Syrup

- 64g golden caster sugar
- 1 tsp rose water
- 3 pieces of lemon zest
- 1 cinnamon stick
- 3 tsp raw honey

The long history and origin of baklava is a much contested one. However, it is generally accepted that it came from the Assyrian empire around 800 BC where layers of thin bread dough baked with chopped nuts and honey were used to celebrate special occasions. Today, Baklava is arguably one of the most popular sweet desserts of Greek, Turkish, Israeli, Lebanese, and Arabic cuisines.

Our little cups of Baklava delights are a sassy take on "cupturing" (capturing) the jam-packed flavours of the baklava into a low carb/low sugar and gluten-free tiny bite, hence making the prefect substitute to a traditionally guilt-filled and sugar laden dessert.

To start, preheat oven 200°C / 180°C fan / gas 6. Grab a mini muffin tin or cupcake tin and spray well with cooking oil or butter it well. Mix the dough ingredients in a bowl. Make sure the butter and cream cheese are soft and at room temperature. Roll and mix all the ingredients into a dough. Spoon out 20 balls of dough and press them into the muffin or cupcake tin to shape them into little delightful cups.

Combine all the nut filling ingredients and fill each of the little cups full of the exquisite mixture. Bake for 20–22 minutes until the dough is golden. Cool to room temperature.

To make the syrup, combine the sugar, rose water, lemon zest, and cinnamon stick in a small saucepan. Cook over medium-low until it simmers. Reduce heat to low and simmer for 5 minutes for the ingredients to get to know each other warmly. Cool to room temperature. Drizzle the magnificent syrup over the cookie cups. To add to the opulence, you can spoon the raw honey over the cup to give it a shimmering glitter. Remove from the tin and enjoy! You can store the cookies in an airtight container but there might not be that many left!

The favourite dessert of Roger Camrass

START COOKING

As we have witnessed in every chapter of the second edition of the CIONET Cookbook, a new digital landscape is emerging at an unprecedented speed. Within this environment, our Master Chefs are being placed centre stage in the business as a revolution plays out.

Given recent unexpected macro-economic and geopolitical events, and the continuing rapid pace of technological developments, we can be certain that further, radical change will come. No one can predict with certainty how world events will unfold during the next year, never mind 20 or even 10 years from now. However, whatever happens next, we already know that the corporate world of the future will be very different to the one we all grew up in.

So, how do we as leaders and active participants in this revolution navigate safe passage for our families, colleagues, organizations, and nations in these turbulent times? At CIONET, we have a deep belief in the power of the community to assist in this endeavour. Across almost two decades, we have established leading communities of practice in 25 countries across Asia, Europe, and the Americas. With the active support of our national advisory boards, we have built a flourishing community of 10,000 technology executives.

The power of this community of practice lies in the constant interaction between our members. CIONET holds more than 350 community events annually, ranging from roundtable events and national community programmes to large international gatherings, including CIONEXT and CIOFEST. Our members testify to us that this constant sharing of experience and best practice has helped to elevate the CIO role to full parity with those positions held by their C-suite peers.

Every year, we undertake "deep dive" TV interviews with 50 of Europe's most influential digital leaders. We publish these interviews on YouTube. These personal stories provide the community with unique and valuable insights into the DNA of its most accomplished Master Chefs. They also help our business partners engage more effectively with IT leaders at the highest levels of their organisations. We encourage you to watch these interviews on the CIONET TV YouTube channel.

In addition, we undertake a constant stream of research programmes to capture and document the insights that arise from our community events and executive interviews. This Cookbook is just one outcome of our research. We hope that you will take full advantage of the many other reports that we publish each year in areas spanning technology strategy, innovative methods, and tools.

In conclusion, we hope that by reading our Cookbook and tasting its successful recipes you will be better equipped to deal with the many challenges and opportunities ahead of you on the journey to becoming digital. As we continue to capture and document recipes from digital leaders—especially via CIONET TV and our many events—we plan to publish further editions of this book as we travel through a unique moment of digital development. In this respect, we acknowledge our gratitude to Red Hat and Intel for sponsoring this second edition of the Cookbook.

We thank you for your interest and participation in this exciting adventure and encourage you to join us at our many local and global events during 2023.

ABOUT THE AUTHORS

Roger Camrass

A pioneer of today's Internet at MIT in the early seventies, Roger has spent over fifty years helping global corporations harness the power of digital technologies such as Cloud, Mobile, Voice Recognition, and Space networks. He led a strategic study—"Business in the Third Millennium"—whilst at SRI and was a senior partner at EY responsible for e-commerce during the dot.com boom. He is now director of research for CIONET International. Roger is a graduate of Cambridge University and MIT, and the author of numerous papers and books. Visit www.rogercamrass.com.

Mark Samuels, Chief Editor

Mark is a business writer and editor, with extensive experience of the way technology is used and adopted by CIOs. His experience has been gained through senior editorships, investigative journalism, and postgraduate research. Editorial clients include the Guardian, The Times, The Sunday Times and the Economist Intelligence Unit. Mark has written content for a range of IT companies and marketing agencies. He has a Ph.D. from the University of Sheffield, and master's and undergraduate degrees in geography from the University of Birmingham. Visit marksamuels.co.uk.

Jenniffer Gearheart-Tang

Jenniffer has over 25 years of international experience specialising in Innovation, Brand Marketing, Market Research, and Senior Executive Recruitment at Shell International, Korn/Ferry International, and Research International.

As Head of Global Innovation & Research at Shell, Jenniffer defined the blueprint for using new and emerging technologies to future proof the business and build a talent and innovation pipeline. One of her key achievements was creating an award-winning global digital platform—Shell Ideas360—which attracted over 62 million views and participation from 140 countries.

As Managing Director of !nnov8 Ltd, Jenniffer has coached over 100 start-up founders, helping them conceptualise products, develop go-to-market strategies, collaborate with and connect to corporations, and to scale their businesses internationally. Visit www.i-nnov8.com.

ABOUT CIONET

CIONET is the leading community of 10,000 senior digital and IT executives in more than 20 countries across Asia, Europe, and the Americas. Through this global community, CIONET helps orchestrate peer-to-peer interactions focused on the most important business and technology issues of the day. CIONET holds over a thousand international and regional live and virtual events annually, ranging from roundtables, community events, and tribe meetings to large international gatherings, including CIONEXT and CIOFEST. Our members testify that CIONET is an impartial and value-adding platform that helps each member advance their professional development and accelerate beneficial outcomes within their organisations.

For more information, please visit www.cionet.com or follow us on LinkedIn and YouTube.

ABOUT THE SPONSORS

About Intel

Intel (Nasdaq: INTC) is an industry leader, creating world-changing technology that enables global progress and enriches lives. Inspired by Moore's Law, Intel continuously works to advance the design and manufacturing of semiconductors to help address their customers' greatest challenges. By embedding intelligence in the cloud, network, edge, and every kind of computing device, Intel unleashes the potential of data to transform business and society for the better. To learn more about Intel's innovations, go to newsroom.intel.com and intel.com.

About Red Hat

Red Hat is the world's leading provider of enterprise open-source software solutions, using a community-powered approach to deliver reliable and high-performing Linux, hybrid cloud, container, and Kubernetes technologies. Red Hat helps customers integrate new and existing IT applications, develop cloud-native applications, standardize on our industry-leading operating system, and automate, secure, and manage complex environments. Award-winning support, training, and consulting services make Red Hat a trusted adviser to the Fortune 500. As a strategic partner to cloud providers, system integrators, application vendors, customers, and open-source communities, Red Hat can help organisations prepare for the digital future.

INDEX

PHOTO CREDITS

page xiii by Louis Hansel on Unsplash
page 2 by Taylor Kiser on Unsplash
page 6 by Oleksandr Kurchev on Unsplash
page 9 by Ulrike Leone on Pixabay
page 11 by micheile dot com on Unsplash
page 12 by Carissa Rogers on Pixabay
page 14 by Ulrike Leone on Pixabay
page 15 by Jonathan Borba on Unsplash
page 17 by Roberta Sorge on Unsplash
page 18 by Nikita Tikhomirov on Unsplash
page 21 by Leo Roza on Unsplash
page 23 by Andrea on Pixabay
page 26 by Jaspreet Kalsi on Unsplash
page 29 by Aline Ponce on Pixabay
page 32 by Lawrence Suzara on Pexels
page 34 by Nathan Dumlao on Unsplash
page 37 by istetiana on Shutterstock
page 40 by Steve Buissinne on Pixabay
page 46 by Gabriel Gurrola on Unsplash
page 51 by Roman Odintsov on Pexels
page 54 by Jirayu Koontholjinda on Unsplash
page 57 by Louis Hansel on Unsplash
page 60 by Duane Mendes on Unsplash
page 63 by Jorge Zapata on Unsplash
page 65 by Rene Lehmkuhl on Pixabay
page 67 by Bartosz Luczak on Dreamstime
page 69 by Nick Karvounis on Unsplash
page 72 by Steve Buissinne on Pixabay
page 74 by Andreas Lischka on Pixabay
page 76 by Louis Hansel on Unsplash
page 79 by Josephine Baran on Unsplash
page 83 by J MAD on Pexels
page 86 by Kelsey Knight on Unsplash
page 89 by Alex Lvrs on Unsplash
page 92 by Stefan Johnson on Unsplash
page 98 by The Matter of Food on Unsplash
page 101 by Tjana Drndarski on Unsplash
page 103 by Anjelagr on Dreamstime
page 106 by NordWood Themes on Unsplash
page 109 by Rod Long on Unsplash
page 111 by Slashio Photography on Unsplash
page 113 by Rohan G on Unsplash
page 117 by -Rita- und mit on Pixabay
page 119 by Carlos Lindner on Unsplash
page 121 by Fabrizio Magoni on Unsplash
page 122 by Kayleigh Harrington on Unsplash
page 124 by Louis Hansel on Unsplash
page 127 by Kasemsan Chamrasamee on iStockphoto
page 129 by Mareefe on Pixabay
page 132 by Rick Bella on Pixabay
page 134 by Svetlana Berdnik on Pixabay
page 136 by Kresopix on iStockphoto
page 138 by Gaelle Marcel on Unsplash
page 142 by Klaus Nielsen on Pexels
page 147 by Softdreams on Dreamstime
page 149 by Loes Klinker on Unsplash